Data-Centric Applications with Vaadin 8

Develop and maintain high-quality web applications using Vaadin

Alejandro Duarte

BIRMINGHAM - MUMBAI

Data-Centric Applications with Vaadin 8

Acquisition Editor: Noyonika Das
Content Development Editor: Mohammed Yusuf Imaratwale
Technical Editor: Shweta Jadhav
Copy Editor: Safis Editing
Project Coordinator: Hardik Bhinde
Proofreader: Safis Editing
Indexer: Mariammal Chettiyar
Graphics: Jason Monteiro
Production Coordinator: Shantanu Zagade

First published: April 2018

Production reference: 1260418

Published by Packt Publishing Ltd.
Livery Place
35 Livery Street
Birmingham
B3 2PB, UK.

ISBN 978-1-78328-884-7

www.packtpub.com

To my mother. Simply, thank you, for everything.

– Alejandro Duarte

`mapt.io`

Mapt is an online digital library that gives you full access to over 5,000 books and videos, as well as industry leading tools to help you plan your personal development and advance your career. For more information, please visit our website.

Why subscribe?

- Spend less time learning and more time coding with practical eBooks and Videos from over 4,000 industry professionals

- Improve your learning with Skill Plans built especially for you

- Get a free eBook or video every month

- Mapt is fully searchable

- Copy and paste, print, and bookmark content

PacktPub.com

Did you know that Packt offers eBook versions of every book published, with PDF and ePub files available? You can upgrade to the eBook version at `www.PacktPub.com` and as a print book customer, you are entitled to a discount on the eBook copy. Get in touch with us at `service@packtpub.com` for more details.

At `www.PacktPub.com`, you can also read a collection of free technical articles, sign up for a range of free newsletters, and receive exclusive discounts and offers on Packt books and eBooks.

Foreword

When introducing Vaadin to a Java developer for the first time, I have often described it as the frontend framework for the backend developer. While this is an oversimplification, most people with little experience on the frontend tend to learn Vaadin quickly and are able to build beautiful web applications with it. I believe this is due to two distinctive properties of Vaadin: one can write the whole web application in server-side Java, and the user interface components look good and feature-rich by default.

If you feel at home writing server-side Java and working with databases, but get frustrated when building the user interface in JavaScript and HTML, this book is for you. Although you need to know the fundamentals of Vaadin, the book starts with the basic concepts and introduces everything you need to become productive at building a data-centric web applications. The approach in the book is practical, showing you by example how to solve the most common challenges and getting you ready for learning more as you go.

Alejandro Duarte would be a great guide for introducing any technology, and we are very fortunate that he joined the Vaadin team after publishing his first book on Vaadin. I hope this book inspires you to build amazing web apps in no time. For questions not discussed in this book, I invite you to join the friendly Vaadin community and share your experiences with other developers who are eager to guide you further.

Joonas Lehtinen

Founder and CEO of Vaadin

Contributors

About the author

Alejandro Duarte is a developer advocate and trainer at Vaadin Ltd. He is also the author of *Vaadin 7 UI Design by Example: Beginner's Guide (Packt,* 2013). Graduating from the National University of Colombia with a B.S. in computer science, Alejandro learned how to program with the BASIC programming language at age 13 and has worked on many software development projects in startup-like and big companies in several countries. When he isn't coding, he splits his time between his family, his beautiful girlfriend, and his passion for the electric guitar. You can follow him on Twitter at *@alejandro_du.*

I'd like to thank the teams at Packt Publishing and Vaadin. Special thanks to Joonas Lehtinen, Sami Ekblad, Matti Tahvonen, and Marcus Hellberg, who in one way or another influenced this book. Thanks to my friends in Finland and Colombia for their motivation. Last but not least, thanks to my parents and siblings for being so supportive; I genuinely enjoyed writing part of this book with your company.

About the reviewer

David Hofmann is a self-taught developer who started working right after high school. 14 years down the lane, he can't help but keep enjoying it. Negotiating and management are the new challenges he finds somewhat more complex than coding, yet much more powerful when delivering solutions. Playing guitar as a hobby keeps him calm, and coffee manages to do the opposite.

Packt is searching for authors like you

Table of Contents

Preface

Vaadin Framework is an open source Java web framework released under the Apache License. The framework is well documented, includes sophisticated UI components and themes, has been battle-tested in real-life applications, and is supported by a committed company and a vibrant community that contributes to the framework through forum answers and hundreds of add-ons.

Vaadin Framework allows developers to implement web user interfaces using Java code that runs on the server's JVM. The UI is rendered as HTML5 on the browser. The framework provides fully automated communication between the browser and the server through a programming model close to Swing or AWT. This allows developers/programmers bringing the benefits of object-oriented techniques to the presentation layer in web applications.

Data-Centric Applications with Vaadin 8 is a practical guide that teaches you how to implement some of the most typical requirements in web applications where data management is central. You will learn about internationalization, authentication, authorization, database connectivity, CRUD views, report generation, and lazy loading of data.

This book will also help you to exercise your programming and software design skills by showing you how to make good decisions both at the UX and code level. You will learn how to modularize your application and how to provide APIs on top of your UI components to increase reusability and maintainability.

Who this book is for

This book is ideal for developers with a good understanding of the Java programming language and a basic knowledge of Vaadin Framework who want to improve their skills with the framework. If you want to learn concepts, techniques, technologies, and practices to help you master web development with Vaadin and see how common application features are developed in real-life applications, this book is for you.

What this book covers

Chapter 1, *Creating New Vaadin Projects*, demonstrates how to create a new Vaadin Maven project from scratch and explains the main architecture and parts of a Vaadin application.

Chapter 2, *Modularization and Main Screens*, explains how to design an API for implementing main screens and shows how to create functional application modules that are registered at runtime.

Chapter 3, *Implementing Server-Side Components with Internationalization*, discusses implementation strategies for implementing custom UI components with internationalization support.

Chapter 4, *Implementing Authentication and Authorization*, explores different approaches for implementing secure authentication and authorization mechanisms in Vaadin applications.

Chapter 5, *Connecting to SQL Databases Using JDBC*, focuses on JDBC, connection pools, and repository classes in order to connect to SQL databases.

Chapter 6, *Connecting to SQL Databases Using ORM Frameworks*, outlines how to use JPA, MyBatis, and jOOQ to connect to SQL databases from Vaadin applications.

Chapter 7, *Implementing CRUD User Interfaces*, takes you through user interface design and the implementation of CRUD (create, read, update, and delete) views.

Chapter 8, *Adding Reporting Capabilities*, shows how to generate and visualize print-preview reports using JasperReports.

Chapter 9, *Lazy Loading*, looks at how to implement lazy loading to make your applications consume fewer resources when dealing with large datasets.

To get the most out of this book

You'll get the most out of this book if you already have some kind of experience with the Vaadin Framework. If you don't, go through the official online tutorial at `https://vaadin.com/docs/v8/framework/tutorial.html` before continuing with this book.

In order to use the companion code, you need the Java SE Development Kit and Java EE SDK version 8 or later. You also need Maven version 3 or later. A Java IDE with Maven support, such as IntelliJ IDEA, Eclipse, or NetBeans is recommended.

Download the example code files

You can download the example code files for this book from your account at www.packtpub.com. If you purchased this book elsewhere, you can visit www.packtpub.com/support and register to have the files emailed directly to you.

You can download the code files by following these steps:

1. Log in or register at www.packtpub.com.
2. Select the **SUPPORT** tab.
3. Click on **Code Downloads & Errata**.
4. Enter the name of the book in the **Search** box and follow the onscreen instructions.

Once the file is downloaded, please make sure that you unzip or extract the folder using the latest version of:

- WinRAR/7-Zip for Windows
- Zipeg/iZip/UnRarX for Mac
- 7-Zip/PeaZip for Linux

The code bundle for the book is also hosted on GitHub at https://github.com/PacktPublishing/Data-Centric-Applications-with-Vaadin-8. In case there's an update to the code, it will be updated on the existing GitHub repository.

We also have other code bundles from our rich catalog of books and videos available at https://github.com/PacktPublishing/. Check them out!

Download the color images

We also provide a PDF file that has color images of the screenshots/diagrams used in this book. You can download it here: http://www.packtpub.com/sites/default/files/downloads/DataCentricApplicationswithVaadin8_ColorImages.pdf.

Code in Action

Visit the following link to check out videos of the code being run:
https://goo.gl/qFmc3L

Conventions used

There are a number of text conventions used throughout this book.

CodeInText: Indicates code words in text, database table names, folder names, filenames, file extensions, pathnames, dummy URLs, user input, and Twitter handles. Here is an example: "The application should be available at http://localhost:8080."

A block of code is set as follows:

```
LoginForm loginForm = new LoginForm()
loginForm.addLoginListener(e -> {
    String password = e.getLoginParameter("password");
    String username = e.getLoginParameter("username");
    ...
});
```

When we wish to draw your attention to a particular part of a code block, the relevant lines or items are set in bold:

```
LoginForm loginForm = new LoginForm() {
    @Override
    protected Component createContent(TextField username,
            PasswordField password, Button loginButton) {

        CheckBox rememberMe = new CheckBox();
        rememberMe.setCaption("Remember me");

        return new VerticalLayout(username, password, loginButton,
                rememberMe);
    }
};
```

Any command-line input or output is written as follows:

```
cd Data-centric-Applications-with-Vaadin-8
mvn install
```

Bold: Indicates a new term, an important word, or words that you see onscreen. For example, words in menus or dialog boxes appear in the text like this. Here is an example: "Select **System info** from the **Administration** panel."

Warnings or important notes appear like this.

 Tips and tricks appear like this.

Get in touch

Feedback from our readers is always welcome.

General feedback: Email `feedback@packtpub.com` and mention the book title in the subject of your message. If you have questions about any aspect of this book, please email us at `questions@packtpub.com`.

Errata: Although we have taken every care to ensure the accuracy of our content, mistakes do happen. If you have found a mistake in this book, we would be grateful if you would report this to us. Please visit `www.packtpub.com/submit-errata`, selecting your book, clicking on the Errata Submission Form link, and entering the details.

Piracy: If you come across any illegal copies of our works in any form on the Internet, we would be grateful if you would provide us with the location address or website name. Please contact us at `copyright@packtpub.com` with a link to the material.

If you are interested in becoming an author: If there is a topic that you have expertise in and you are interested in either writing or contributing to a book, please visit `authors.packtpub.com`.

Reviews

Please leave a review. Once you have read and used this book, why not leave a review on the site that you purchased it from? Potential readers can then see and use your unbiased opinion to make purchase decisions, we at Packt can understand what you think about our products, and our authors can see your feedback on their book. Thank you!

For more information about Packt, please visit `packtpub.com`.

Creating New Vaadin Projects

This first chapter serves as the foundations for a journey full of interesting technologies, thrilling challenges, and useful code. If you are reading this book, the chances that you have coded a Vaadin application before are high. You probably have a basic understanding of the key players in a Vaadin application: components, layouts, listeners, binders, resources, themes, and widget sets; and you, of course, have had your share of Java coding!

Having a solid base when starting a project, not only with Vaadin but with any other technology, plays an important role in successful projects. Understanding what your code does and why it is required helps you make better decisions and become more productive. This chapter will help you understand what is really needed to run a Vaadin application and how you can become more confident about the dependencies and Maven configuration required to start a new Vaadin project.

This chapter covers the following topics:

- The main Java dependencies in Vaadin
- Servlets and UIs
- Maven plugins
- Key elements in a Vaadin application

Technical requirements

You will be required to have Java SE Development Kit and Java EE SDK version 8 or later. You also need Maven version 3 or later. A Java IDE with Maven support, such as IntelliJ IDEA, Eclipse, or NetBeans is recommended. Finally, to use the Git repository of this book, you need to install Git.

The code files of this chapter can be found on GitHub:
`https://github.com/PacktPublishing/Data-centric-Applications-with-Vaadin-8/tree/master/chapter-01`

Check out the following video to see the code in action:
`https://goo.gl/RHavBs`

About the demo applications

This book offers value in two ways: the book itself with its explanations, and its companion source code. Instead of developing one single application throughout the book, several small demo applications demonstrate the concepts explained in each chapter. This helps you to jump to any chapter you are interested in, and fully understand the purpose of each part of the code without worrying about the technicalities that we have looked at in other chapters.

Understanding the source code

Before you compile the project, you have to start an H2 database instance. For your convenience, a server is configured in the `Data-centric-Applications-with-Vaadin-8/chapter-05` Maven module. You can create a run configuration for the following Maven command or you can run it directly on the command line:

```
cd Data-centric-Applications-with-Vaadin-8/chapter-05
mvn test exec:java -
Dexec.mainClass="packt.vaadin.datacentric.chapter05.jdbc.H2Server"
```

Once the database is up and running, you can build all the demo applications by executing the following:

```
cd Data-centric-Applications-with-Vaadin-8
mvn install
```

All the demo applications are aggregated in a multi-module Maven project, where each module corresponds to one chapter of the book.

 This book assumes that you are proficient enough with Maven to follow the example applications of each chapter. If you have no previous experience with Maven or multi-module Maven projects, please spend some time going through the tutorials and documentation at: `http://maven.apache.org/guides`.

Each chapter's module may contain multiple sub-modules depending on the concepts being explained in that chapter. We will use the Jetty Maven plugin to run the examples. Most IDEs today have good support for Maven. The best way to use this book's code is by importing the `Data-centric-Applications-with-Vaadin-8` Maven project into your IDE and creating individual *running configurations* for each demo application. There are tons of resources online that explain how to do this for the most popular IDEs, such as IntelliJ IDEA, NetBeans, and Eclipse. For example, to run the example application for this chapter in IntelliJ IDEA, create a new running configuration like the following:

Make sure the working directory corresponds to the correct module in the project. Alternatively, you can run the application by executing the following on the command line:

```
cd Data-centric-Applications-with-Vaadin-8/chapter-01
mvn package jetty:run
```

This executes the package Maven phase and starts a Jetty server. The application should be available at `http://localhost:8080`.

So, go ahead! Download the source code, import it into your IDE, and run a couple of examples. Feel free to explore the code, modify it, and even use it in your own projects.

Understanding the architecture of a Vaadin application

What's the best way of starting a new Vaadin project? It's hard to say. It depends on your previous experience, current development environment setup, and your own preferences. One of the most popular ways of creating a new Vaadin project is by using one of the official *Maven archetypes*. You have probably used the `vaadin-archetype-application` Maven archetype, which is good to quickly get started with Vaadin. Maybe you have used the `vaadin-archetype-widgetset` archetype to create a Vaadin add-on, or maybe you have used the `vaadin-archetype-application-multimodule` or `vaadin-archetype-application-example` archetypes to bootstrap some of your applications. IDEs such as Eclipse provide tools to create a Vaadin project without even thinking about Maven archetypes.

All of those archetypes and tools are good in the sense that they get you started quickly and show some good practices. However, when you create a project from scratch, you get a better understanding of the whole architecture of the application. Of course, you can use the archetypes if you already feel comfortable enough with every part of the generated `pom.xml` file. However, building the project from scratch is a good way of truly understanding and controlling the configuration of your Vaadin application.

Creating a new project from scratch

Usually, you would use the `vaadin-archetype-application` or `vaadin-archetype-application-multimodule` Maven archetypes to create a new Vaadin application. There's nothing wrong with using these if the generated code suits your needs. However, these archetypes generate more code than you need, partially because they try to show you how to get started with Vaadin and partially because they are general-purpose starters which are well-suited for most projects. But let's gain full control (and understanding) of the web application by creating a Vaadin project in a very different way—a more fine-grained, controlled way.

A Vaadin application is, at the end of the day, a Java application packaged as a WAR file. You can think of it as a standard web application in which you drop some JARs that allow you to build a web UI using the Java Programming Language instead of HTML and JavaScript. Is it as simple as dropping some JARs into your Java project? Let's find out!

Use the maven-archetype-webapp to generate a simple Java web application by executing the following on the command line:

```
mvn archetype:generate –DarchetypeGroupId=org.apache.maven.archetypes –
DarchetypeArtifactId=maven-archetype-webapp
```

Use the following properties when prompted:

- groupId: packt.vaadin.datacentric.chapter01
- artifactId: chapter-01
- version: 1.0-SNAPSHOT
- package: packt.vaadin.datacentric.chapter01

IDEs such as NetBeans, Eclipse, and IntelliJ IDEA have excellent support for Maven. You should be able to create a new Maven project using the previous archetype in your IDE by providing the corresponding Maven coordinates without using the command line.

Clean up the pom.xml file to make it look like the following:

```
<project ...>
    <modelVersion>4.0.0</modelVersion>

    <artifactId>chapter-01</artifactId>
    <version>1.0-SNAPSHOT</version>
    <packaging>war</packaging>
</project>
```

Note that in the code provided with this book, you'll find a <parent> section in the pom.xml file of the chapter-01 project. This is because all the demo applications of the book have been aggregated into a single Data-centric-Applications-with-Vaadin-8 Maven project for your convenience. You don't need to add any <parent> section to your project if you are following the steps in this chapter.

Remove the `src/main/webapp` and `src/main/resources` directories. This deletes the generated `web.xml` file which will make Maven complain. To tell it that this was intended, add the following property to your `pom.xml` file:

```
...
<packaging>war</packaging>
<properties>
    <failOnMissingWebXml>false</failOnMissingWebXml>
</properties>
...
```

Also, add the following properties to configure Maven to use Java 8:

```
<maven.compiler.source>1.8</maven.compiler.source>
<maven.compiler.target>1.8</maven.compiler.target>
```

Maven dependencies

At this point, we have a very simple Java project setup that will be packaged as a WAR file. The next natural step is to add the required dependencies or libraries. Vaadin, like many other Java web applications, requires the Servlet API. Add it as follows to the `pom.xml` file:

```
<dependencies>
    <dependency>
        <groupId>javax.servlet</groupId>
        <artifactId>javax.servlet-api</artifactId>
        <version>3.1.0</version>
        <scope>provided</scope>
    </dependency>
</dependencies>
```

Notice that the scope of this dependency is set as `provided`, which means that a server, or more specifically, a Servlet Container, such as Jetty or Tomcat, will provide the implementation.

Let's continue by adding the required Vaadin dependencies. First, add the `vaadin-bom` dependency to your `pom.xml` file:

```
<dependencyManagement>
    <dependencies>
        <dependency>
            <groupId>com.vaadin</groupId>
            <artifactId>vaadin-bom</artifactId>
            <version>8.3.2</version>
            <type>pom</type>
```

```
        <scope>import</scope>
      </dependency>
    </dependencies>
  </dependencyManagement>
```

 This book uses Vaadin Framework version 8.3.2, the latest production-ready version of the framework at the time of writing.

A Maven BOM, or bill of materials, frees you from worrying about versions of related dependencies; in this case, the Vaadin dependencies. Let's drop these dependencies next. Add the following to your pom.xml file:

```
<dependency>
    <groupId>com.vaadin</groupId>
    <artifactId>vaadin-server</artifactId>
</dependency>
<dependency>
    <groupId>com.vaadin</groupId>
    <artifactId>vaadin-client-compiled</artifactId>
</dependency>
<dependency>
    <groupId>com.vaadin</groupId>
    <artifactId>vaadin-themes</artifactId>
</dependency>
```

There's no need to explicitly set the version for these thanks to the vaadin-bom dependency. We've just added a server-side API (vaadin-server), a client-side engine or widget set (vaadin-client-compiled), and the Valo theme (vaadin-themes).

At this point, you can compile the project by running the following command inside the chapter-01 directory:

```
mvn clean install
```

This will download the dependencies to your local Maven repository if you haven't used Vaadin 8.3.2 before.

Servlets and UIs

A Vaadin application in its simplest form is a `Servlet` that delegates user interface logic to a `UI` implementation. The `vaadin-server` dependency includes the `Servlet` implementation: the `VaadinServlet` class. Let's configure one.

Create a new directory with the name `java` inside the `src/main` directory.

 You might have to tell your IDE that this is a source directory. You will most likely find this by right-clicking the directory and selecting the option to mark it as a source directory. Check the documentation for your IDE for detailed instructions.

Create a new package with the name `packt.vaadin.datacentric.chapter01`, and add a simple `UI` implementation inside this package:

```
public class VaadinUI extends UI {

    @Override
    protected void init(VaadinRequest vaadinRequest) {
        setContent(new Label("Welcome to Data-Centric Applications with
Vaadin 8!"));
    }
}
```

Add a new `WebConfig` class to encapsulate everything related to web configuration, and define the `VaadinServlet` as an inner class:

```
public class WebConfig {

    @WebServlet("/*")
    @VaadinServletConfiguration(
            ui = VaadinUI.class, productionMode = false)
    public static class WebappVaadinServlet extends VaadinServlet {
    }
}
```

The `WebappVaadinServlet` class must be `public static` to allow its instantiation by the Servlet Container. Notice how we are configuring `/*` as the servlet URL mapping using the `@WebServlet` annotation. This makes the application available at the root of the deployment path. Notice also how the `@VaadinServletConfiguration` annotation connects the `Servlet` to the `UI` implementation, the `VaadinUI` class we implemented in the previous step.

Maven plugins

You must have used, or at least seen, the Vaadin Maven plugin. It allows you to compile the widget set and theme, among other tasks. When creating a new Vaadin application, though, you don't have any add-ons, custom client-side components, or themes. This means you don't need the Vaadin Maven plugin just yet. You can use the default widget set provided by the `vaadin-client-compiled` dependency.

We can benefit from at least one Maven plugin at this point: the Jetty Maven plugin. Although you can configure most IDEs to use a variety of servers in order to deploy your application during development, the Jetty Maven plugin frees you from further specific configurations, making it simple for developers to choose the tools they prefer. To use the plugin, add the following to the `pom.xml` file:

```xml
<build>
    <plugins>
        <plugin>
            <groupId>org.eclipse.jetty</groupId>
            <artifactId>jetty-maven-plugin</artifactId>
            <version>9.3.7.v20160115</version>
        </plugin>
    </plugins>
</build>
```

With this in place, you can run the application by creating a new running configuration in your IDE to execute `mvn jetty:run`. Point your browser to `http://localhost:8080` and you should see the application running:

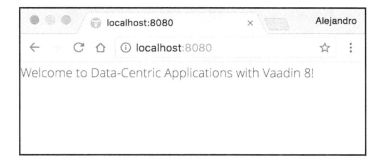

Components and layouts

To get a full picture of the main parts of a Vaadin application, let's do a quick review of some of the most important classes you should already be familiar with. In a Vaadin application, most of the code deals with components and layouts. In a nutshell, you add components such as `Label`, `TextField`, `CheckBox`, `ComboBox`, and `Grid` into layouts such as `VerticalLayout`, `FormLayout`, `GridLayout`, `HorizontalLayout`, and `CSSLayout`. You can also add layouts into layouts.

 During design or development, you might want to explore the available components and layouts in the framework so that you can pick the best for a particular scenario. One way to see all the components and layouts included in the framework is by visiting the Vaadin sampler at: `http://demo.vaadin.com/sampler`. You can see code examples by clicking the **Information** icon in the upper right corner of the page:

```
Information                                    ⚙  ⓘ  ☰

                                  Description        Source

1.     private final Command menuCommand = selectedItem -> Notification.show("Action " + select
2.
3.  ...
4.
5.         sample = new MenuBar();
6.         sample.setWidth(100.0f, Unit.PERCENTAGE);
7.
8.  ...
9.
10.            final MenuItem child;
11.            if (parent == null) {
12.                child = sample.addItem(caption, command);
13.            } else {
14.                child = parent.addItem(caption, command);
15.                if (addSeparator) {
16.                    parent.addSeparatorBefore(child);
17.                }
18.            }
19.
20.            child.setEnabled(enabled);
21.            child.setIcon(icon);
```

Listeners and binders

Vaadin applications interact with the server through listeners and binders. Listeners allow you to handle user interaction, while binders allow you to keep values in input components (such as `TextField`) and domain objects (for example, a custom `User` class) in sync.

Events and listeners

In a Vaadin application, the behavior is added through *listeners*. A listener fires an event when the corresponding action happens, usually caused by the interaction of the user with the UI. Two of the most common listeners in Vaadin are `ClickListener` (for buttons) and `ValueChangeListener` (for input components). Listeners are usually defined by implementing a *functional interface*, which allows you to react to an event using a method reference:

```
protected void init(VaadinRequest vaadinRequest) {
    Button button = new Button("Click this");
    button.addClickListener(this::buttonClicked);
}
...
private void buttonClicked(Button.ClickEvent event) {
    Notification.show("Thanks for clicking");
}
```

You can also use a Lambda expression instead:

```
button.addClickListener(
        event -> Notification.show("Thanks for clicking"));
```

And to make it more readable and testable, extract the listener logic to a new method, passing only what's needed as parameters (in this case, nothing is needed):

```
protected void init(VaadinRequest vaadinRequest) {
    ...
    button.addClickListener(event -> buttonClicked());
}
...
private void buttonClicked() {
    Notification.show("Thanks for clicking");
}
```

Data binding

Data binding is typically done through the `Binder` class. This class allows you to connect the values in one or more fields to Java properties in a domain class. Suppose you have a `User` class (the domain class) with a `password` Java `String` as one of its properties. You can create a `TextField` and bind its value to the `password` property as follows:

```
TextField textField = new TextField("Email");
Binder binder = new Binder<User>()
    .forField(textField)
    .bind(User::getPassword, User::setPassword);
```

This is a powerful and type-safe way of implementing data binding. Imagine that you, at some point during development, decide to rename the `password` property in the `User` class to something like `pin`. You can use the refactoring tools of your IDE to rename the property, and the IDE will rename the getters, setters, and any code calling these two methods. Of course, you'd have to change the caption `"Email"` to `"PIN"` yourself, but that would have also been the case with other binding mechanisms.

Binders are also used to add validators and converters. These can be added using Lambda expressions or method references. For example, the following snippet of code checks that a `String` has exactly 4 characters and converts it into an integer:

```
binder.withValidator(s -> s.length() == 4, "Must be 4 characters")
    .withConverter(Integer::parseInt, Object::toString);
```

Resources and themes

The `Resource` interface and its implementations are the connections between Java code and resources such as images, downloadable files, or embedded content. You have probably used a `StreamResource` to dynamically generate a file that a user can download or a `ThemeResource` to display an image in your UI.

A theme, in turn, is a set of static resources used to configure the appearance of a Vaadin application. By default, Vaadin applications use the Valo theme, a powerful set of styles that can be configured using variables.

Widget sets and add-ons

So far, you have been introduced to the most common parts of a Vaadin application. Vaadin is mostly about using an API with Java running on the server side. This Java code defines how the application looks and behaves, but a Vaadin application runs on a browser using HTML 5 and JavaScript. You don't have to write a line of HTML or JavaScript in order to implement a Vaadin application. How is this possible? How does a Java class define the HTML rendered in the browser?

The key to understanding this is the *widget set*. A widget set is a JavaScript engine running on the client side, which contains all the code required to show components and communicate with the server side. A widget set is generated by compiling a set of Java classes into JavaScript using GWT. These Java classes are provided by the Vaadin Framework and you can add your own if you want to. If you are not using custom client-side components (your own, or those provided by a third-party Vaadin add-on), you can use the already compiled widget set which is included in the `vaadin-client-compiled` dependency.

Summary

This chapter served as an introduction to the architecture of a Vaadin application and its main players. We explained the most important parts of a Vaadin application and how they are connected. We also learned how to create a minimal Vaadin application from scratch by adding every single configuration required by ourselves.

In the next chapter, you will learn how to implement main screens and custom application modules that are discovered and registered with a Vaadin application at runtime.

2
Modularization and Main Screens

The main purpose of modularization is to decrease the complexity of a system. By dividing the functionality into many modules, developers can *forget* about parts of the system that are not relevant to the functionality under development. It also enables a more powerful deployment process by, for example, allowing activation of features depending on environments or customers, and the creation of third-party modules to customize and extend the capabilities of the application.

This chapter demonstrates how to modularize your applications to make them more manageable and maintainable, and how to implement a main screen that supports the registration of new modules at runtime.

This chapter covers the following topics:

- Modularization of Vaadin applications
- Implementation of an application's main screens

Technical requirements

You will be required to have Java SE Development Kit and Java EE SDK version 8 or later. You also need Maven version 3 or later. A Java IDE with Maven support, such as IntelliJ IDEA, Eclipse, or NetBeans is recommended. Finally, to use the Git repository of this book, you need to install Git.

The code files of this chapter can be found on GitHub:
https://github.com/PacktPublishing/Data-centric-Applications-with-Vaadin-8/tree/master/chapter-02

Check out the following video to see the code in action:
`https://goo.gl/VnLouE`

Creating a multi-module Maven project

A *multi-module* Maven project aggregates several Maven projects into a single one. In this chapter, we will create three modules that form the whole application:

- `webapp`: A Vaadin web application packaged as a WAR file that includes everything needed to deploy it to a server such as Tomcat, Wildfly, Jetty, or any other Java server
- `api`: A Java API packaged as a JAR used by the webapp and any *functional module*
- `example-module`: An example *functional module* that uses the `api` JAR to add functionality to the application

All these modules are aggregated into a single Maven project with the name `chapter-02`. Let's start by creating this aggregator project by using the `pom-root` Maven archetype. Run the following in a terminal:

```
mvn archetype:generate \
-DarchetypeGroupId=org.codehaus.mojo.archetypes \
-DarchetypeArtifactId=pom-root \
-DarchetypeVersion=RELEASE
```

Use the following properties when prompted:

- `groupId`: `packt.vaadin.datacentric`
- `artifactId`: `chapter-02`
- `version`: `1.0-SNAPSHOT`
- `package`: `packt.vaadin.datacentric.chapter02`

When using this archetype, Maven generates a `pom.xml` file for a top-level multi-module or aggregator project. You can remove the `<name>` tag as it's redundant for our purposes. Modify the file to include a property for the Vaadin version:

```
<project xmlns="..." xsi:schemaLocation="...">
    <modelVersion>4.0.0</modelVersion>

    <groupId>packt.vaadin.datacentric</groupId>
    <artifactId>chapter-02</artifactId>
    <version>1.0-SNAPSHOT</version>
```

```
<packaging>pom</packaging>

<properties>
    <vaadin.version>8.3.2</vaadin.version>
</properties>
</project>
```

 Note that in the code provided with this book, you'll find a `<parent>` section in the `pom.xml` file of the `chapter-02` project. This is because all the demo applications of the book have been aggregated into a single `Data-centric-Applications-with-Vaadin-8` Maven project for your convenience. You don't need to add any `<parent>` sections to your project if you are following the steps in this chapter.

This project (`chapter-02`) can be seen as the root directory for a full-blown application that contains several Maven modules, each one dedicated to a specific aspect of the functionality of the system.

Implementing an application's main screen

Let's start by implementing a concrete component: A main screen, something every web application needs. Please keep in mind that there's not only one way of implementing main screens. The example presented here may be good for your own application, or it might inspire you to develop even more sophisticated implementations.

The main screen in this example consists of a *header*, a *menu*, and a *working area* where other components are shown when the user selects an option from the main menu. To the external world, this component should include the following functionality:

- Adding components to the header
- Adding components to the working area
- Adding options to the main menu
- Adding listeners to respond to menu actions
- Getting components from the working area and the header

Defining an API for an application's main screen

In order to explore and learn about API design in web development with Vaadin, let's assume we want the main screen to be a general purpose component not intended to be used only in this demo application. For this reason, we need to provide the component in a separate JAR file. Start by creating a new Maven module inside the chapter-02 project using the maven-archetype-simple archetype as follows:

```
cd chapter-02
mvn archetype:generate -DarchetypeGroupId=org.apache.maven.archetypes -
DarchetypeArtifactId=maven-archetype-quickstart
```

Use the following properties when prompted:

- groupId: packt.vaadin.datacentric.chapter02
- artifactId: api
- version: 1.0-SNAPSHOT
- package: packt.vaadin.datacentric.chapter02.api

Check that the new api module is listed in the chapter-02/pom.xml file:

```
<project ...>
    ...
    <modules>
        <module>api</module>
    </modules>
</project>
```

Clean up as desired and add the Vaadin BOM and the vaadin-server dependency. You can also delete the generated App and AppTest classes. You will also need to configure Java 8 using properties, similar to how it was done in the previous chapter.

 You can find the full pom.xml file in the Data-centric-Applications-with-Vaadin-8\chapter-02\api Maven project of the source code that accompanies this book.

The API should allow developers to create additional concrete main screen implementations with similar functionality. Abstracting this functionality can be done by defining a Java interface like the following:

```
public interface ApplicationLayout extends Component {

  void addHeaderComponent(Component component);

  void addWorkingAreaComponent(WorkingAreaComponent
        component);

  Collection<Component> getHeaderComponents();

  Collection< WorkingAreaComponent> getWorkingAreaComponents();

  void addMenuOption(MenuOption menuOption,
        SerializableConsumer<MenuOption> clickListener);

}
```

 The ApplicationLayout interface and related classes are located in the Data-centric-Applications-with-Vaadin-8/chapter-02/api Maven project of the source code that accompanies this book.

This interface extends Component, so any concrete implementation can be used as a regular UI component and added into any Vaadin component container, such as VerticalLayout, for instance. Concrete implementations will extend Composite, as will be shown later.

Implementing support classes

The previous interface won't compile. There are two classes that need to be implemented: WorkingAreaComponent and MenuOption. The addWorkingAreaComponent(WorkingAreaComponent) method expects a WorkingAreaComponent that encapsulates a caption and the corresponding Vaadin component to be shown. This interface is defined as follows:

```
public interface ApplicationLayout extends Component {

    public static class WorkingAreaComponent
            implements Serializable {

        private final String caption;
        private final Component component;
```

```
public WorkingAreaComponent(String caption,
        Component component) {
    this.caption = caption;
    this.component = component;
}

... hashCode(), equals(), and getters
}
...
}
```

The WorkingAreaComponent class implements Serializable. Vaadin is mostly a server-side framework. Components are stored in HTTP sessions. In order to serialize the session, all contained objects must be Serializable. This serialization is done, for example, when you stop a web container such as Jetty or Tomcat. All HTTP sessions are serialized to the disk, and the next time the server starts, sessions are restored. Notice also how SerializableConsumer was used in the ApplicationLayout interface for the same reasons.

Why is that needed? Why not simply let the addWorkingAreaComponent(WorkingAreaComponent) method have the parameters for the caption and component, as shown in the following snippet of code?

```
void addWorkingAreaComponent(String caption, Component component);
```

If you were a hundred percent sure that a caption and a component are the only things you need to have when you add a new component to the working area, that would be fine. However, you don't know how concrete ApplicationLayouts will evolve. What if an icon is needed? What about a color or a help text?

Suppose you have decided to implement the method as addWorkingAreaComponent(String, Component) and some months after the component is released, some application that uses the component needs to have an icon for each component added into the working area. A possible solution is to modify the method to accept a new parameter for the icon, as follows:

```
void addWorkingAreaComponent(String caption, Component component,
        Resource icon);
```

This modification will break any existing client that references the old method's signature. Another approach is to overload the method by adding a new parameter. However, this will break all current implementations of `ApplicationLayout`. Encapsulating what is subject to change is always a good idea.

Another reason to encapsulate the parameters of `addWorkingAreaComponent(WorkingAreaComponent)` is the `getWorkingAreaComponents()` method. Suppose you want to implement a concrete `ApplicationLayout` that allows users to switch between tabs and windows. In order to implement this functionality, you need to get all the current components shown in the working area (using the `getWorkingAreaComponents(WorkingAreaComponent)` method) and place them in tabs or windows accordingly. For each component, you need to create a tab or a window, set its caption, and add the corresponding Vaadin component. You need both, the caption and the component. Encapsulating these objects in a single class greatly simplifies this task; otherwise, we would need to have an extra method that returns the captions as an ordered collection. Additionally, the `getWorkingAreaComponents()` method should return an ordered collection as well.

The last thing to notice about the `ApplicationLayout` class is the `addMenuOption(MenuOption, SerializableConsumer<MenuOption>)` method. This method expects a `MenuOption` (that encapsulates the caption to render) and a `SerializableConsumer` that serves as a click listener for the menu option. When the user clicks the option, the `Consumer.accept(MenuOption)` method is called, passing the clicked `MenuOption` as its parameter.

> `SerializableConsumer` is a serializable version of the `Consumer` class, a functional interface introduced in Java 8. A functional interface has only one abstract method. This allows clients to create instances of the interface using lambda expressions. For more information about functional interfaces see: `http://docs.oracle.com/javase/8/docs/api/java/lang/FunctionalInterface.html`.

The `MenuOption` class can be implemented as follows:

```
public interface ApplicationLayout extends Component {

    public static class MenuOption implements Serializable {
        private final String caption;

        public MenuOption(String caption) {
            this.caption = caption;
        }
```

```
        public String getCaption() {
            return caption;
        }
    }
}
```

Implementing a concrete application's main screen

This section explains how to implement and use a basic tab-based layout using the `ApplicationLayout` interface developed in the previous section. The layout includes a header on the top and a lateral menu on the left. When users click an option on the main menu a new component is added inside a new tab. The following is a screenshot of this layout:

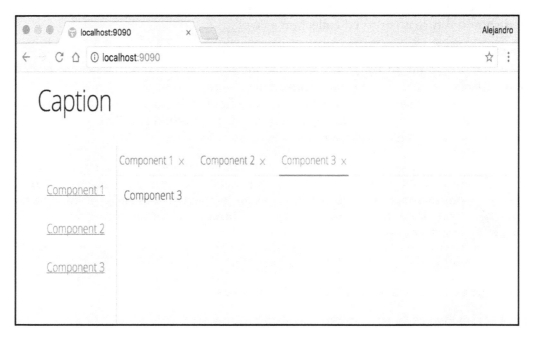

Adding and configuring the required UI components

The first step is to create the required Vaadin UI components and configure them using the standard Vaadin API. This can be done as follows:

```
public class TabBasedApplicationLayout extends Composite {

    private VerticalLayout mainLayout = new VerticalLayout();
    private HorizontalLayout header = new HorizontalLayout();
    private HorizontalSplitPanel splitPanel
            = new HorizontalSplitPanel();
    private VerticalLayout menuLayout = new VerticalLayout();
    private TabSheet tabSheet = new TabSheet();

    public TabBasedApplicationLayout(String caption) {
        ... layout and components configuration
    }
}
```

The code to configure the UI elements is omitted, as it is not the purpose of this book to explain Vaadin UI components' basic usage and configuration. The full implementation can be found in the `Data-centric-Applications-with-Vaadin-8\chapter-02\api` **Maven** project of the source code that accompanies this book.

Implementing the ApplicationLayout interface

The next step is to implement the `ApplicationLayout` interface and add the required methods:

- `void addHeaderComponent(Component)`
- `void addWorkingAreaComponent(WorkingAreaComponent)`
- `Collection<Component> getHeaderComponents()`
- `Collection<WorkingAreaComponent> getWorkingAreaComponents()`
- `void addMenuOption(MenuOption, SerializableConsumer<MenuOption>)`

Implementing the `addHeaderComponent(Component)` method is quite straightforward:

```
@Override
public void addHeaderComponent(Component component) {
    component.setWidth(null);
    header.addComponent(component);
```

```
            header.setComponentAlignment(component,
                Alignment.MIDDLE_RIGHT);
    }
```

The `addWorkingAreaComponent(WorkingAreaComponent)` method should avoid adding two tabs with the same caption. Instead of adding the same tab twice it should select the corresponding existing tab. A `Collection` is used to keep track of the added components, as shown in the following code:

```
    public class TabBasedApplicationLayout extends CustomComponent
            implements ApplicationLayout {
        ...

        private Collection<WorkingAreaComponent> workingAreaComponents
            = new HashSet<>();

        @Override
        public void addWorkingAreaComponent(WorkingAreaComponent
                component) {
            addWorkingAreaComponent(component, true);
        }

        public void addWorkingAreaComponent(WorkingAreaComponent
                component, boolean closable) {
            if (!workingAreaComponents.contains(component)) {
                TabSheet.Tab tab = tabSheet.addTab(
                        component.getComponent(),
                            component.getCaption());
                tab.setClosable(closable);
                tabSheet.setSelectedTab(tab);
                workingAreaComponents.add(component);
            } else {
                showComponent(component.getCaption());
            }
        }

        public void showComponent(String caption) {
            IntStream.range(0, tabSheet.getComponentCount())
                    .mapToObj(tabSheet::getTab)
                    .filter(tab -> tab.getCaption().equals(caption))
                    .forEach(tabSheet::setSelectedTab);
        }
    }
```

Because this concrete implementation is based on a `TabSheet` where each tab can or cannot be closed, it makes sense to overload the `ApplicationLayout.addWorkingAreaComponent(WorkingAreaComponent)` method to allow clients to specify this behavior.

An interesting part of the previous code is the `showComponent(String)` method, which selects a tab by its caption. This method uses an `IntStream` to loop through the tabs in the `TabSheet`. This method is equivalent to the following one:

```
public void showComponent(String caption) {
    for(int i = 0; i < tabSheet.getComponentCount(); i++) {
        TabSheet.Tab tab = tabSheet.getTab(i);

        if(tab.getCaption().equals(caption)) {
            tabSheet.setSelectedTab(tab);
        }
    }
}
```

> The implementation of `showComponents(String)` uses two Java 8 features called streams and pipelines. For more information on streams and pipelines,
> see http://docs.oracle.com/javase/tutorial/collections/streams/index.html.

The next method to implement is `getHeaderComponents()`:

```
@Override
public Collection<Component> getHeaderComponents() {
    return IntStream.range(0, header.getComponentCount())
            .mapToObj(header::getComponent)
            .collect(Collectors.toList());
}
```

This method uses an `IntStream` similar to the one in the `showComponent(String)` method. A `Collector` is used to create a `List` containing all the components in the header.

Since we already have a `Collection` object with all the components in the working area, the `getWorkingAreaComponents()` method implementation is just a regular getter:

```
@Override
public Collection<WorkingAreaComponent> getWorkingAreaComponents() {
    return workingAreaComponents;
}
```

Implementing the menu

To make the menu work, we can implement the addMenuOption(MenuOption, SerializableConsumer<MenuOption>) method as follows:

```
public class TabBasedApplicationLayout ... {
    ...
    private Collection<String> menuButtonStyles = new HashSet<>();
    ...

    @Override
    public void addMenuOption(MenuOption menuOption,
            SerializableConsumer<MenuOption> clickListener) {
        Button button = new Button(menuOption.getCaption(),
                event -> clickListener.accept(menuOption));
        menuButtonStyles.forEach(button::addStyleName);
        menuLayout.addComponent(button);
    }
    ...
}
```

This method iterates over the menuButtonStyles collection to add each style to the new button. Lastly, the methods to set styles for menu options and also for the header should look as follows:

```
public void setHeaderStyleName(String styleName) {
    header.setStyleName(styleName);
}

public void addHeaderStyleName(String styleName) {
    header.addStyleName(styleName);
}

public void setMenuButtonsStyleName(String styleName) {
    menuButtonStyles.clear();
    menuButtonStyles.add(styleName);
    updateMenuButtonsStyle(styleName,
            Component::setStyleName);
}

public void addMenuButtonsStyleName(String styleName) {
    menuButtonStyles.add(styleName);
    updateMenuButtonsStyle(styleName,
            Component::addStyleName);
}

private void updateMenuButtonsStyle(String styleName,
```

```
        BiConsumer<Component, String> setOrAddStyleMethod) {
    IntStream.range(0, menuLayout.getComponentCount())
            .mapToObj(menuLayout::getComponent)
            .forEach(component ->
                    setOrAddStyleMethod.accept(
                            component, styleName));
}
```

The component is now ready! We can use it in any Vaadin application now. You can create a Vaadin application in a similar way as we did in the previous chapter, or use a standard Vaadin Maven archetype. The chapter-02 module includes the webapp submodule, a Vaadin web application. The following is the init method of the UI implementation in the webapp module:

```
protected void init(VaadinRequest request) {
    TabBasedApplicationLayout layout =
            new TabBasedApplicationLayout("Caption");
    IntStream.range(1, 4)
            .mapToObj(i -> new Label("Component " + i))
            .map(l -> new ApplicationLayout.WorkingAreaComponent(
                    l.getValue(), l))
            .forEach(c -> layout.addMenuOption(
                    new ApplicationLayout.MenuOption(
                            c.getCaption()),
                    (option) ->
                            layout.addWorkingAreaComponent(
                                    c, true)));
    layout.setMenuButtonsStyleName(ValoTheme.BUTTON_LINK);
    setContent(layout);
}
```

Remember to add the api dependency to the pom.xml file of the webapp module before compiling and running the application again:

```
<dependency>
    <groupId>packt.vaadin.datacentric.chapter02</groupId>
    <artifactId>api</artifactId>
    <version>1.0-SNAPSHOT</version>
</dependency>
```

Although we have learned how to build a bare-bones main screen in the previous sections by using the core of Vaadin Framework, you should consider using the *SideMenu Add-on* published in the Vaadin Directory website (`https://vaadin.com/directory/component/sidemenu-add-on`). This component allows you to quickly implement side menus like the one in the official *dashboard demo* you can see at `https://demo.vaadin.com/dashboard`.

Modularizing Vaadin applications

In this book, we use the term module to refer to a software component that can be independently developed and deployed. In that sense, a modularized application can be customized and extended without distributing or modifying the source code of the original application. For our purposes, when a new module is deployed, it must register with the application. The functionality of the module is incorporated into the application at runtime.

 Keep in mind that there are also Maven modules. This book uses the full term Maven module or Maven project when referring to this kind of modules.

Identifying alternatives for modularization

There are several mechanisms and ways of implementing modularized applications in Java. For example, you can use OSGi if you need to provide hot deployment—that is, the capability of deploying and un-deploying modules at runtime. Another option is **Service Provider Interface** (**SPI**), a set of standard interfaces and classes included in Java SE that help with the development of extensible applications. You can even use **Contexts and Dependency Injection** (**CDI**) or an *inversion of control* framework such as the one provided by the Spring Framework to develop a custom module system based on the injection mechanism. Moreover, you could go down to the Java Reflection API to create instances of classes not known at compile time.

Because explaining all these alternatives is out of the scope of this book, we'll use the simplest alternative: SPI.

Registering modules with the application

Registering a module with the application means adding the module's functionality into the application. What this module registration performs depends on the application's requirements. For example, if the application includes a main menu, then a possible registration action for a module is to add menu items to the main menu. If the application is based on tabs, a possible registration action can be adding tabs to the main screen. All these actions need to be performed through a shared API. Take the example of adding a menu item. In this case, a possible interface could be something like the following:

```
public interface MenuItemRegistration {
    void addMenuItem(MenuBar menu);
}
```

Modules can implement this interface to add menu items into the existing application's main menu.

Because we already have an `ApplicationLayout` interface, which defines methods to manipulate the layout, the following interface is good enough:

```
public interface AppModule {
    void register(ApplicationLayout layout);
}
```

 The `AppModule` interface is located in the `Data-centric-Applications-with-Vaadin-8\chapter-02\api` Maven project of the source code that accompanies this book.

This interface can be packaged in a separate JAR file so it can be distributed to any third-party developers. This JAR should contain all the classes and interfaces that could be needed by module implementations. This is the reason we previously created the `api` Maven module. There also is another advantage: The `api` JAR can be distributed to third-party developers to allow them to create new functionality for the application without distributing the whole compiled code of your web application.

Discovering modules

The webapp application should detect all the implementations of AppModule at run-time. For each implementation, it should create a new instance and call the register(ApplicationLayout) method. Doing this with Java SPI is surprisingly simple:

```
public class VaadinUI extends UI {

    protected void init(VaadinRequest vaadinRequest) {
        TabBasedApplicationLayout layout
            = new TabBasedApplicationLayout("Caption");
        setContent(layout);
        loadModules(layout);
    }

    private void loadModules(
            ApplicationLayout applicationLayout) {
        ServiceLoader<AppModule> moduleLoader =
                ServiceLoader.load(AppModule.class);
        moduleLoader.forEach(
                module -> module.register(applicationLayout));
    }
}
```

The ServiceLoader class is used to discover all the classes that implement the AppModule interface. For each module, we call its register method, passing the layout of the application to give the module the chance to initialize itself and modify the layout if required.

Implementing new modules

New modules have to implement the AppModule interface and follow the SPI requirements for packaging by adding a new file with the name packt.vaadin.datacentric.chapter02.api.AppModule into the META-INF/services directory. This file must contain the name of the fully qualified name of the AppModule implementation.

Let's say you want to develop a module that adds an option to the main menu that shows a notification when clicked. This can be easily implemented as follows:

```
package com.example;
...

public class ExampleModule implements AppModule {

    @Override
    public void register(ApplicationLayout layout) {
        ApplicationLayout.MenuOption menuOption
            = new ApplicationLayout.MenuOption("Example module");
        layout.addMenuOption(menuOption, this::optionClicked);
    }

    private void optionClicked(
                ApplicationLayout.MenuOption menuOption) {
        Notification.show("It works!",
            Notification.Type.TRAY_NOTIFICATION);
    }
}
```

This class can be located in a separate Maven project and should include the `api` dependency.

 The `ExampleModule` implementation is located in the `Data-centric-Applications-with-Vaadin-8\chapter-02\example-module` **Maven** project of the source code that accompanies this book.

To make the module discoverable by the `webapp` application, you must add a file with the name `packt.vaadin.datacentric.chapter02.api.AppModule` in the `main/resources/META-INF/services` directory of the new module. The file must contain the fully-qualified name of the `AppModule` implementation as follows:

```
packt.vaadin.datacentric.chapter02.example.module.ExampleModule
```

Once packaged, you can deploy the JAR file independently and the `webapp` application should automatically discover and register the module.

To deploy a module with the web application, you can add it as a dependency in the pom.xml file of the Data-centric-Applications-with-Vaadin-8/chapter-02/webapp Maven project. If you are deploying the application as a WAR file to a servlet container, you can add the JAR to the WEB-INF/lib directory.

The following is a screenshot of the application, showing the example module in action:

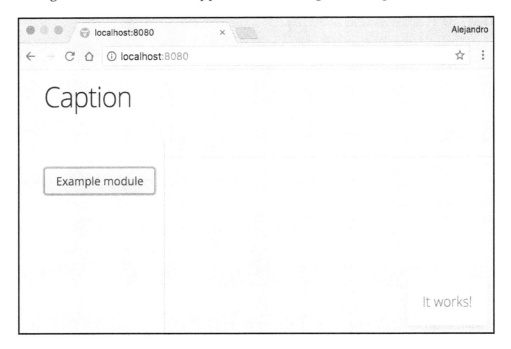

Summary

In this chapter, we developed a self-packaged UI component (a *main screen* component), created a multi-module Maven project, and learned how to implement application-specific modules that are discovered and registered with a Vaadin application at run-time. While explaining these concepts, we also saw some Java 8 and Vaadin 8 snippets of code that highlighted good practices such as making your code more maintainable and extensible.

In the next chapter, you will learn how to implement a login form with multi-language capabilities.

3
Implementing Server-Side Components with Internationalization

Having a login form is arguably one of the most common requirements in web applications. In this chapter, you will learn how to implement a reusable and extensible login form that supports multiple languages, and see the advantages of favoring *composition* over *extension* when implementing UI components. Through examples, we'll discuss why *extension* is not always the best approach, and we'll explore several alternatives for implementing custom server-side UI components with Vaadin.

This chapter covers the following topics:

- Extending layout components
- Using the `Composite` class
- Externalization of Java Strings

Technical requirements

You will be required to have Java SE Development Kit and Java EE SDK version 8 or later. You also need Maven version 3 or later. A Java IDE with Maven support, such as IntelliJ IDEA, Eclipse, or NetBeans is recommended. Finally, to use the Git repository of this book, you need to install Git.

The code files of this chapter can be found on GitHub:
`https://github.com/PacktPublishing/Data-centric-Applications-with-Vaadin-8/tree/master/chapter-03`

Check out the following video to see the code in action:
`https://goo.gl/fu8W3W`

Using extensions to develop a UI component

Let's explore how to implement a login form component. The first idea that comes to mind when starting to develop a UI component is to extend, in the Java sense, an existing component. Most of the time, the natural choice is to extend a layout component such as `VerticalLayout` or `HorizontalLayout`. For example, a login form usually includes at least a **username** field, a **password** field, a **login** button, and a **remember me** checkbox, with all of them aligned vertically. So, let's start by directly extending `VerticalLayout`.

Extending VerticalLayout

The following snippet of code shows a typical way of extending `VerticalLayout` to implement a UI component, in this case, the login form:

```
public class LoginFormLayout extends VerticalLayout {

    private TextField username = new PasswordField();
    private PasswordField password = new PasswordField();
    private Button logIn = new Button();
    private CheckBox rememberMe = new CheckBox();

    public LoginFormLayout() {
        ...
        addComponents(username, password, logIn, rememberMe);
    }
    ...
}
```

The logic to handle events and additional UI configuration that might be required is omitted in the previous example.

The full implementation of the `LoginFormLayout` class is located in the `Data-centric-Applications-with-Vaadin-8/chapter-03` Maven project of the source code that accompanies this book.

Why avoid extension?

What is wrong with the previous implementation? Well, there's nothing inherently wrong with it. However, it can be highly improved. The LoginFormLayout class violates encapsulation! Clients of the class know that a VerticalLayout is used. All public methods of VerticalLayout are exposed to clients of LoginFormLayout. If, for some reason, the implementation needs to change to a different layout (a FormLayout, CssLayout, or even a Panel, for instance), clients calling any method in VerticalLayout that are not in the new base layout class would break.

To the outside world, LoginFormLayout is a Layout. The purpose of a login form is not to serve as a layout (to position other components), but to show the fields that are required to authenticate users with the application. So, let's try to get more encapsulation into the design!

Using composition to develop custom components

If extending VerticalLayout is a problem, a possible solution is to not extend any class at all. However, in that case, we wouldn't get a Component, but a class of which instances cannot be added to the components tree. What about extending a more suitable component in the hierarchy? Let's start with interfaces. The following figure shows some of the top interfaces in the hierarchy:

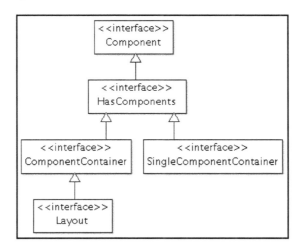

Going up the hierarchy, we find the `Component` interface which has more than 20 methods that would require an implementation. The other interfaces inherit these 20+ methods and add some more. Fortunately, Vaadin provides abstract implementations for these interfaces. The following figure shows some of the equivalent implementations:

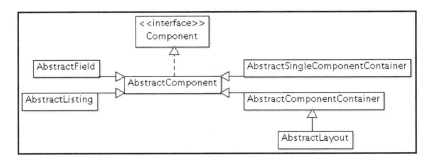

`AbstractComponent` is the default implementation of `Component`. Many Vaadin components directly extend this class. It's not a convenient class for the login form, though, since it's too general and doesn't offer methods to add other components to it. `AbstractField` and `AbstractListing` can be discarded as well because the login form is not just a field showing a value or a list of values, respectively.

The next candidates are the `AbstractSingleComponentContainer`, `AbstractComponentContainer`, and `AbstractLayout` classes. These classes help with the implementation of layouts, but as we discussed previously, a login form shouldn't look like a layout to the external world.

Implementing a factory

How about a factory of components? The following is an implementation of a factory with a method that returns a `Component`:

```
public class LoginFormFactory {

    public static Component getComponent() {

        ... create and configure all required components

        return new VerticalLayout(
                username, password, button, rememberMe);
    }
}
```

This hides the implementation details but also makes it more difficult and complex to offer functionality to the clients. For example, how would clients of the class get the username or password values introduced by the user in the form? One option is to implement getters in the factory class, but that would require some more adjustments in the `LoginFormFactory` class. At the end of the day, this kind of implementation would require you to implement (and maintain) two highly coupled classes for a single custom component. Not a very good idea.

Using the Composite class

If you have some experience with Vaadin, chances are that you already know the `CustomComponent` class. The `Composite` class works in the same way as the `CustomComponent` class, but it's more lightweight since it only adds a simple `<div>` element to the DOM in the browser. The `Composite` class eases the development of compositions of components by eliminating some of the problems previously described. `Composite` directly extends `AbstractComponent`, which means that any class extending `Composite` is a `Component` itself that can be added to any Vaadin layout. A `Composite` can specify a composition root that serves as the root of the components tree (usually a layout), for example:

```
public class LoginFormComponent extends Composite {

    public LoginFormComponent() {

        ... create and configure all required components

        VerticalLayout layout = new VerticalLayout(
                username, password, button, rememberMe);

        setCompositionRoot(layout);
    }

    ... getters and setters
}
```

Using the LoginForm class

Vaadin comes with a `LoginForm` class that, by default, renders a username and a password field. It also adds *auto-completion* and *auto-fill* in the browser. The `LoginForm` class is a good candidate for extension (and you have to extend it if you want to override its defaults). For example, the following snippet of code creates a `loginForm` and a listener that is invoked when the user clicks the **login** button:

```
LoginForm loginForm = new LoginForm()
loginForm.addLoginListener(e ->  {
    String password = e.getLoginParameter("password");
    String username = e.getLoginParameter("username");
    ...
});
```

To add more fields to the form, override the `createContent` method. For example:

```
LoginForm loginForm = new LoginForm() {
    @Override
    protected Component createContent(TextField username,
            PasswordField password, Button loginButton) {

        CheckBox rememberMe = new CheckBox();
        rememberMe.setCaption("Remember me");

        return new VerticalLayout(username, password, loginButton,
            rememberMe);
    }
};
```

Despite its design for extension, it's always a good idea to hide implementation details by extending `Composite` and abstracting away the underlying `LoginForm` class. The following snippet of code shows a first iteration of the new `LoginFormComponent` class:

```
public class LoginFormComponent extends Composite {

    private TextField username;
    private PasswordField password;
    private CheckBox rememberMe = new CheckBox();

    public LoginFormComponent() {
        LoginForm loginForm = new LoginForm() {
            @Override
            protected Component createContent(TextField username,
                    PasswordField password, Button loginButton) {
                LoginFormComponent.this.username = userNameField;
```

```
            LoginFormComponent.this.password = passwordField;

            rememberMe.setCaption("Remember me");

            return new VerticalLayout(username,password,
                    loginButton, rememberMe);
        }
    };

    setCompositionRoot(loginForm);
    }
}
```

The createContent method is called internally by the LoginForm class. Notice how the username and password variables are assigned to references in the LoginFormComponent class. These references can be used later to retrieve the values in the fields.

Allowing clients of the LoginFormComponent class to be notified when the user clicks the **login** button can be implemented with a custom LoginListener interface:

```
public class LoginFormComponent extends Composite {

    public interface LoginListener {
        void logInClicked(LoginFormComponent loginForm);
    }
    ...

    private LoginListener loginListener;

    public LoginFormComponent(LoginListener loginListener) {
        this();
        this.loginListener = loginListener;
    }

    public LoginFormComponent() {
        ...

        loginForm.addLoginListener(this::logInClicked);
        ...
    }

    public void setLoginListener(LoginListener loginListener) {
        this.loginListener = loginListener;
    }

    private void logInClicked(LoginForm.LoginEvent loginEvent) {
```

```
        if (loginListener != null) {
            loginListener.logInClicked(this);
        }
    }
}
```

The `LoginListener` interface defines one method that accepts a `LoginFormComponent`. Now, it's easy to define getters to allow clients to obtain the values in the fields:

```
public class LoginFormComponent extends Composite {
    ...

    public String getUsername() {
        return username.getValue();
    }

    public String getPassword() {
        return password.getValue();
    }

    public boolean isRememberMe() {
        return rememberMe.getValue();
    }
}
```

If a new component is added to the login form in future, it's possible to add a getter to return the value in the added field without breaking existing clients of the class.

The final version of the `LoginFormComponent` class can be found in the `Data-centric-Applications-with-Vaadin-8\chapter-03` Maven project of the source code that accompanies this book.

Using internationalization for Multiple Language Support

Internationalization is the process of making an application ready to support several languages and data formats. An internationalized application can be adapted for a particular language and region, a process known as *localization*, which consists of adding a specific set of resources (usually text, images, and data formats) to an internationalized application. Ideally, localization should not require rebuilding the application, but only adding the localized resources and, at most, restarting the web container.

Addressing internationalization early in a software development project and knowing the audience makes the process much easier. Internationalization is orthogonal to all the application layers, and the process of localizing can involve translating and defining several resources such as texts, images, videos, audio files, number formats, date formats, currency symbols, and even colors.

Removing hardcoded strings

Custom reusable UI components should not depend on the mechanism used to handle internationalization. The LoginFormComponent, for instance, should include setters (or alternatively, parameters in the constructor) to configure the captions of the inner UI components. The following implementation shows how to use setters to configure captions in the login form:

```java
public class LoginFormComponent extends Composite {
    ...

    private String usernameCaption = "Username";
    private String passwordCaption = "Password";
    private String loginButtonCaption = "Log in";
    private String rememberMeCaption = "Remember me";

    public LoginFormComponent() {
        LoginForm loginForm = new LoginForm() {
            @Override
            protected Component createContent(...) {
                username.setPlaceholder(usernameCaption);
                password.setPlaceholder(passwordCaption);
                loginButton.setCaption(loginButtonCaption);
                rememberMe.setCaption(rememberMeCaption);
                ...
            }
        };

        ...
    }

    public void setUsernameCaption(String usernameCaption) {
        this.usernameCaption = usernameCaption;
    }

    ... similar setters for password, login, and remember me ...
}
```

It's a good idea to provide defaults and a method to set all the captions in one call. The implementation in the example application includes such features.

Getting localized strings

At this point, the LoginFormComponent can be internationalized. The next step is to pass the strings containing the captions in the correct language. Usually, the Locale and ResourceBundle standard Java classes are good enough to externalize localized messages. However, it is also a good idea to isolate string externalization logic into a separate class that allows clients to add resource bundles and get localized strings by name. Encapsulating this logic into a separate class allows you to change the underlying mechanism (for example, to read the messages from a database) and add features such as caching without affecting the rest of the application.

The following is an implementation of the Messages utility class used to encapsulate string externalization logic:

```
public class Messages {

    private static final TreeSet<String> baseNames =
            new TreeSet<>();

    public static void addBundle(String baseName) {
        baseNames.add(baseName);
    }

    public static String get(String key) {
        return baseNames.stream()
                .map(baseName -> ResourceBundle.getBundle(
                        baseName, UI.getCurrent().getLocale()))
                .filter(bundle -> bundle.containsKey(key))
                .map(bundle -> bundle.getString(key))
                .findFirst().get();
    }

}
```

This class can be used to register a *base name* used internally by the standard `ResourceBundle` class. This base name should match the name of the properties files with the translations. For example, to add English and Spanish messages, you have to create two files, `messages_en.properties` and `messages_es.properties`. The `messages` part in the name of these files corresponds to the *base name*. You can load these resource bundles by calling `Messages.addBundle("messages")`.

> The `Messages` class is located in the `Data-centric-Applications-with-Vaadin-8\chapter-03` Maven project of the source code that accompanies this book. The class includes a method to get all the available languages that you can use to allow end users to change the language from the UI.

Supporting a new language is as easy (or complicated) as adding a new `.properties` file (in the `resources` directory) containing the translated properties. For example, a `messages_en.properties` file could define the following properties:

```
auth.username=Username
auth.password=Password
auth.login=Login
auth.rememberMe=Remember me
auth.logout=Logout
auth.bad.credentials=Wrong username or password
```

To support Spanish, for example, you would have to add a `messages_es.properties` file with the following content:

```
auth.username=Usuario
auth.password=Contrase\u00f1a
auth.login=Acceder
auth.rememberMe=Recordarme
auth.logout=Salir
auth.bad.credentials=Usuario o contraseña incorrectos
```

> Note that you have to use *unicode scape syntax* if you want to include special characters (like the Spanish *n* with a *tilde* in the example).

You can get a message in the language of the browser by calling `Messages.get("property")`. For example, the following snippet of code sets the correct labels for the components in the `LoginFormComponent`:

```
loginForm.setCaptions(
        Messages.get("auth.username"),
        Messages.get("auth.password"),
        Messages.get("auth.login"),
        Messages.get("auth.rememberMe"));
```

Getting and setting the locale

Vaadin automatically sets the `Locale` reported by the browser. You can get this `Locale` by calling the `UI::getLocale()` method and the `UI::setLocale(Locale)` method to set the `Locale` for the current user. The example application in this chapter uses the locale reported by the browser. There's no need do anything else except add the resource bundle using the helper `Messages` class. The example application does this in a static block in the `UI` implementation (the `VaadinUI` class):

```
static {
    Messages.addBundle("messages");
}
```

In more complex scenarios, you should use an event listener such as `ServletContextListener` to add the resource bundle when the context starts, for example.

You can configure your browser in a different language to test this functionality. How to configure this may depend on your browser and operating system vendor. In Chrome, however, you can use the **Language** settings. Just move the language that you wish to test to the top of the list. You have to restart Chrome for this change to take effect.

The following is a screenshot of the `LoginFormComponent` using the Spanish locale:

 Internationalization requires a constant effort throughout the development of UIs. Try to catch yourself *hard-coding* strings and immediately fix them by creating an entry in the appropriate properties file. Incorporate this practice into your coding routine.

When implementing truly internationalized applications, you should have a well-defined and simple process that allows translators to create all the localizations (translations) for new resources. A way of doing this is by using well-defined directories or files that translators can take and complete (by translating the strings, for example) before a new production-ready artifact is constructed.

Summary

In this chapter, we learned how to design UI components with the help of object-oriented techniques by considering several approaches such as extending layout components, extending a specialized component, and using composition with the help of the `Composite` class. We developed a `LoginForm` class that uses the browser's language to show captions in the appropriate language.

In the next chapter, you will learn how to make the login form functional by adding authentication and authorization capabilities.

4
Implementing Authentication and Authorization

Authentication is the process that ensures the identity of a user, usually done by providing a set of identifying credentials (username and password). Authorization is the security process that determines the access levels a user has in the application. In this chapter, we will continue with the development of the login form implemented in Chapter 3, *Implementing Server-Side Components with Internationalization*, by adding authentication and authorization features. We'll also learn how to implement the *remember me* option in the login form.

This chapter covers the following topics:

- The HTTP session
- Cookies management
- Authorization and authentication mechanisms

Technical requirements

You will be required to have Java SE Development Kit and Java EE SDK version 8 or later. You also need Maven version 3 or later. A Java IDE with Maven support, such as IntelliJ IDEA, Eclipse, or NetBeans is recommended. Finally, to use the Git repository of this book, you need to install Git.

The code files of this chapter can be found on GitHub:
https://github.com/PacktPublishing/Data-centric-Applications-with-Vaadin-8/tree/master/chapter-04

Check out the following video to see the code in action:
https://goo.gl/RM8KNY

Implementing public and private views

Frequently, web applications have two main screens. One for visitors who are not authenticated, and one for users who are authenticated. It makes sense to implement the UI in a way that reflects this exactly. The idea is to create two custom components (using the Composite class); one for public access, and one for authenticated users. So, for now, let's suppose we have a custom PublicComponent class that shows the login form and a PrivateComponent that shows something like the following:

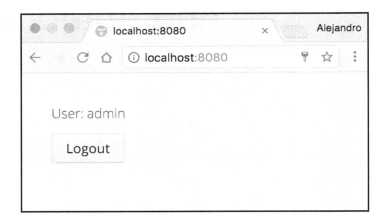

When the user is successfully authenticated, the PrivateComponent is shown. When the **Logout** button is clicked, the user should be redirected to the PublicComponent. The Vaadin UI implementation (VaadinUI in this chapter's example) should reflect the fact that there are two main screens that can be shown depending on whether the user is authenticated or not.

The init method of the UI implementation should verify whether a user is authenticated already, and if so, show the PrivateComponent. Otherwise, it should show the PublicComponent. This is necessary to cover the case when the user reloads the page in the browser: we don't want the user to have to re-authenticate after a page reload. In plain Java, this functionality looks like the following:

```java
public class VaadinUI extends UI {

    static { Messages.addBundle("messages"); }

    @Override
    protected void init(VaadinRequest vaadinRequest) {
        if (AuthService.isAuthenticated()) {
```

```
        setContent(new PrivateComponent());
    } else {
        setContent(new PublicComponent());
    }
  }
}
```

We'll develop the `AuthService` class in a bit, but the point in this section is to show you how simple the `UI` implementation can be. Always try to keep your `UI` implementation simple! Delegate to other classes the actual functionality of your application. Reflect only the essence of the top-level workflow of the application in your `UI` implementation. In our case, a simple class that shows one of two main screens, plus a sensible default depending on the authentication state, is enough.

One of the security features of Vaadin Framework is the fact that, by default, there's no way to access the execution of code by requesting different URLs. In the previous example, requesting `http://localhost:8080` will always invoke the `init` method, which gives us the chance to check whether the user is authenticated or not by asking a service class. You might be wondering how the authentication state is kept on the server. The answer is the HTTP session.

 You can learn more about security in Vaadin Framework applications at `https://vaadin.com/security`.

Using the HTTP session and cookies to identify users

One way of keeping track of the state of a web application is by making use of the HTTP session. The currently authenticated user is part of the state of the application and can be stored in the HTTP session. In Vaadin applications, you can store values in the HTTP session by using the `VaadinSession.setAttribute(String, Object)` method. The first parameter is a custom identifier for the value which is specified using the second parameter. For example, we can store the number `777` in an attribute with the name `number` in the HTTP session as follows:

```
VaadinSession.getCurrent().setAttribute("number", 777);
```

You can remove the value from the session by passing `null`:

```
VaadinSession.getCurrent().setAttribute("number", null);
```

Keeping track of authenticated users

Following this approach, we can store the `username` in the HTTP session when a user is successfully authenticated. We can also check whether the user has been authenticated by checking whether a value exists in the HTTP session. This can be implemented as follows:

```
public class AuthService {

    private static final String USERNAME_ATTRIBUTE = "username";

    public static boolean authenticate(
            String username, String password) {

        boolean authentic = "admin".equals(username) &&
                "admin".equals(password);

        if (authentic) {
            VaadinSession.getCurrent().setAttribute(
                    USERNAME_ATTRIBUTE, username);
        }

        return authentic;
    }

    public static boolean isAuthenticated() {
        return VaadinSession.getCurrent().getAttribute(
                USERNAME_ATTRIBUTE) != null;
    }
}
```

There are a few things to notice here. First, for simplicity in this example, the code checks whether `username` and `password` are both equal to the string `"admin"`. In a real application, this should query a database or delegate to any other authentication process. For example, if you have a class that provides functionality to query user data, the Boolean check could look something like the following:

```
User existingUser = userRepository.findByUsernameAndPassword(
        username, password);
boolean authentic = existingUser != null;
```

Never store passwords in a way that they can be retrieved. In other words, always store *salted hashes* of passwords instead of the password itself. This can protect not only your users but also yourself! If you store a password as a hash of it, you can be sure that nobody, including you, can get to know the real password. If the database is compromised, at least the passwords are going to be garbage. Suppose you have a `hash` method that uses SHA or any other secure algorithm. When setting a password, you can save an entity with something like the following:
`user.setPassword(hash(theActualPassword));`
In order to check whether a password is correct (for example, during authentication), you can compare the hash of the given password with the value stored in the database. Something like the following:

- `String stored = user.getPassword();`
- `String hash = hash(attemptedPassword);`
- `if (stored.equals(hash) {...}`

Second, the `AuthService` class has Vaadin stuff in it. Service classes should be decoupled from the presentation technology, but in our case, that's okay, since there's not much chance of us changing the web framework! And that's usually the case in real-life applications anyway. Additionally, reusing this class out of the context of a Vaadin application doesn't seem very likely, but if it becomes necessary, you can decouple it from Vaadin by directly using the HTTP session.

If your application allows third-party developers to add new functionality to your application and it exposes the HTTP session, developers might be able to impersonate a user if they know their username. Since the only condition for declaring a user as authenticated is to have an entry in the HTTP session with the corresponding username as its key, a malicious developer could add such a username and invoke other functionality on their behalf. In such cases, consider symmetrically encrypting the key (username) or even using an alternative storage mechanism for the HTTP session.

Implementing the login/logout process

Let's recap what we have implemented at this point. We have a multi-language LoginFormComponent ready for use (developed in Chapter 3, *Implementing Server-Side Components with Internationalization*), a UI implementation that shows a PublicComponent or a PrivateComponent, depending on whether a user is authenticated, and an AuthService class that allows us to authenticate a user (if their login credentials are correct) and check whether there is an authenticated user in the session or not.

It's time to complete the login/logout process by implementing the PublicComponent and PrivateComponent classes. Let's start with the PublicComponent class:

```
public class PublicComponent extends Composite {

    public PublicComponent() {
        LoginFormComponent loginForm = new LoginFormComponent();
        loginForm.setCaptions(
                Messages.get("auth.username"),
                Messages.get("auth.password"),
                Messages.get("auth.login"),
                Messages.get("auth.rememberMe"));

        loginForm.setLoginListener(form -> loginClicked(form));
        setCompositionRoot(loginForm);
    }

    private void loginClicked(LoginFormComponent form) {
        if (!AuthService.authenticate(
                form.getUsername(), form.getPassword())) {
            Notification.show(
                    Messages.get("auth.bad.credentials"),
                        Notification.Type.ERROR_MESSAGE);
        }
    }
}
```

This component extends `Composite` and uses the `LoginFormComponent` as its composition root. The `loginClicked` method is called when the user clicks the respective button, and it's inside this method where we try to authenticate the user. If the credentials are correct, we show an error notification, but if they are correct, we are not doing anything at all! And actually, we don't really need to do anything else in this class. Do you remember how we implemented the `VaadinUI` class so that it would show one screen or the other according to the authentication state? Well, all we need to do in order to make this work is add a simple page reload to the `AuthService.authenticate` method for when the authentication succeeds:

```
public class AuthService {

    private static final String USERNAME_ATTRIBUTE = "username";

    public static boolean authenticate(
            String username, String password) {

        boolean authentic = "admin".equals(username) &&
                "admin".equals(password);

        if (authentic) {
            VaadinSession.getCurrent().setAttribute(
                    USERNAME_ATTRIBUTE, username);
            Page.getCurrent().reload();
        }

        return authentic;
    }
    . . .
}
```

That's right! Since the `VaadinUI.init` method is called when the user refreshes the browser and our implementation checks whether there's an authenticated user in the HTTP session (via the `AuthService` class), we don't need to do anything else.

How about the other way around? When the user logs out, we should perform two actions:

1. Remove all the data in the HTTP session (invalidate the session).
2. Refresh the browser (in order to invoke the `VaadinUI.init` method and automatically show the `PublicComponent`).

It's just reasonable to implement this functionality in the `AuthService` class:

```
public class AuthService {
    ...

    public static void logout() {
        VaadinService.getCurrentRequest().getWrappedSession()
                .invalidate();
        Page.getCurrent().setLocation("");
    }
}
```

The `invalidate` method removes any values from the HTTP session and invalidates it. The server will create a new session if the application is requested again.

Servers maintain sessions in several ways, such as through cookies or URL rewriting. Depending on your specific server, you might have to call `VaadinService.reinitializeSession(VaadinService.getCurrentRequest())` to ensure a new session key is generated after you invalidate a session.

Notice how we reloaded the browser this time. Instead of calling the `Page.reload()` method, we are making sure that the URL in the browser requests the starting URL for the web application. This will also remove, for example, any fragments or parameters from the URL that may contain *sensitive information*.

Sensitive information refers to any kind of data, information, or knowledge that must be protected against unauthorized access.

Finally, the `PrivateComponent` class should be pretty straightforward to implement. For the sake of completeness, here's the code:

```
public class PrivateComponent extends Composite {

    public PrivateComponent() {
        Label label = new Label(
                "User: " + AuthService.getAuthenticatedUser());
        Button logOutButton = new Button(
                Messages.get("auth.logout"),e -> logoutClicked());
        setCompositionRoot(new VerticalLayout(label,
                logOutButton));
    }
```

```
private void logoutClicked() {
    AuthService.logout();
}
}
```

Notice the `AuthService.getAuthenticatedUser()` method. You can implement that method with one line of code:

```
public class AuthService {
    ...

    public static String getAuthenticatedUser() {
        return (String) VaadinSession.getCurrent().getAttribute(
            USERNAME_ATTRIBUTE);
    }
}
```

 Remember to use HTTPS (HTTP Secure) any time you have a web application with a login form that sends user credentials through the network. By enabling HTTPS, the data is encrypted, preventing man-in-the-middle attacks. You can learn more about how to enable HTTPS at https://vaadin.com/blog/enabling-https-in-your-java-server-using-a-free-certificate.

Implementing the remember me feature

The *remember me* feature allows users to automatically authenticate themselves with the web application even after they have closed the browser, or the HTTP session has been destroyed, without having to enter their usernames and passwords. If a user has previously authenticated themselves and chose to be remembered, the web application will, remember the user using HTTP cookies.

Essentially, with the *remember me* feature, your application can consume two kinds of *login credentials*:

- A username and password combination
- A valid HTTP cookie previously created by the web application

Let's think of the login/logout process, putting the *remember me* functionality into play this time. When a user requests the web application for the first time, the `VaadinUI.init` method is invoked. This method will check whether the user is authenticated or not in order to show the corresponding `UI` component. This is delegated to the `AuthService` class in our example. The `AuthService.isAuthenticated` method checks whether or not there's an authenticated user in the HTTP session. At first, there is none, so it should check whether the user was *remembered* before. Ignoring the details, we know the user was not remembered before. So the `PublicComponent` is shown and the user can log in with, username and password. But this time, the user checks the **Remember me** checkbox.

We need to tell this choice to the `AuthService.authenticate` method (by passing a Boolean value from the checkbox), which in turn will check if the username and password are correct and, if so, perform the logic to *remember* the user. This is the interesting part.

A user is remembered by creating an HTTP cookie with the name, say `remember-me`, and storing a value that allows us to identify the user later. We could be tempted to simply store the plain username in this cookie, but that would lead to a serious security issue; if a malicious user has access to the browser and gets the value of a `remember-me` cookie, they will be able to sign in as that user by simply creating a cookie with the stolen value.

Instead of storing *sensitive information* in the cookie, we can store a randomly generated string and store the username in the server using a Java `Map`, where the key is the random string and the value is the username.

Using a Java `Map` is good enough for the example in this chapter. However, keep in mind that if you restart the server, remembered users are no longer remembered (pun intended). A real-life application should use a persistent `Map`, such as an SQL table, but the principle is exactly the same. Additionally, you might want to store a hash of the random key, in the same way as you should do with user passwords. This will protect users if data in this table is compromised.

So, let's recap. The user logged in by providing their username and password and checking the **Remember me** option, and the web application created a cookie containing a random key and stored the username in a `Map` using that key. Now, let's see what happens when the user closes the browser (or waits until the HTTP session is closed) and requests the web application again.

As usual, the `VaadinUI.init` method is invoked and the `AuthService.isAuthenticated` method checks whether there's an authenticated user in the HTTP session. Of course, there isn't, and it proceeds with the cookie check. This time, there is a `remember-me` cookie, so the method just searches for the username in the `Map` of remembered users and gets the value of the username. Now, it should just store the username in the HTTP session and return `true`. The user was automatically authenticated!

The last part we need to consider is the logout action. When the user logs out, the `remember-me` cookie should be destroyed, along with the corresponding entry in the Java `Map` of remembered users.

I would urge you to try and implement all this by yourself. I have created a branch with the name `remember-me-exercise` in the source code that accompanies this book. You can use this branch as a starting point if you want to do the exercise. You can check it out by running:

```
cd Data-centric-Applications-with-Vaadin-8
git checkout remember-me-exercise
```

If you prefer to see the solution, just check the code in the `master` branch.

Let's see some snippets of code you could use for the exercise. Let's begin with HTTP cookies management. You can send a new cookie to the browser by using the `VaadinRequest.addCookie` method. The following snippet of code creates a new cookie with the name `remember-me` and the value `admin` and sends it to the browser:

```
Cookie cookie = new Cookie("remember-me", "admin");
cookie.setPath("/");
cookie.setMaxAge(60 * 60 * 24 * 15);
VaadinService.getCurrentResponse().addCookie(cookie);
```

The `setPath` defines the path for the cookie. The browser sends the cookies associated with that path in subsequent requests to the server.

 Note that the path should include the servlet's context path. You can get it by calling `VaadinServlet.getCurrent().getServletContext().getContextPath()`.

The `setMaxAge` method allows you to set the time for which the cookie will be valid. The time is given in seconds, which means that the previous snippet creates a cookie valid for 15 days.

To delete a cookie, set its age to zero. For example, the following code removes the `remember-me` cookie:

```
Cookie cookie = new Cookie("remember-me", "");
cookie.setPath("/");
cookie.setMaxAge(0);
VaadinService.getCurrentResponse().addCookie(cookie);
```

You can get all the cookies reported by the browser by using the `VaadinRequest.getCookies` method. You can get an instance of `VaadinRequest` via `VaadinService.getCurrent()`. The following snippet of code retrieves an `Optional` of a cookie with the name `remember-me`:

```
Cookie[] cookies = VaadinService.getCurrentRequest().getCookies();

Optional<Cookie> cookie = Arrays.stream(cookies)
        .filter(c -> "remember-me".equals(c.getName()))
        .findFirst();
```

Finally, here there's a tip to generate a random string suitable for the `Map` of remembered users:

```
SecureRandom random = new SecureRandom();
String randomKey = new BigInteger(130, random).toString(32);
```

In short, this converts a randomly generated `BigInteger` consisting of 130 bits and converts them into a sequence of base-32 characters. Although 128 bits is secure enough, a base-32 character can take five bits. *128/5 = 25.6*, so we need a couple of extra bits to get the next multiple of 5, which leads to *130/5=26*. In conclusion, we get 26 random characters. Keep in mind that UUIDs are not designed to be unpredictable and should not be used to identify sessions.

A good implementation should also periodically clean the `Map` of remembered users. This can be achieved by adding a custom data type that stores not only the username but the expiry date. A background process can run every day, checking for expired entries and removing them from the `Map`.

Enabling features according to a user's roles

This section discusses authorization implementation strategies. Authorization is the process of granting access to resources according to a defined policy. Keep in mind that *authentication* is the process of verifying if a user or another system is who they claim they are, *authorization* deals with what a certain user can do.

Authorization mechanisms can be implemented in many ways depending on the specific requirements of an application. Some applications use a basic public/private approach (like the one we have used so far in this chapter) where the policy is as simple as checking if a user is authenticated in order to grant access to a certain UI component. Other applications may require multiple roles, each one with a different set of permissions. Moreover, a user may have multiple roles at the same time and those roles could change at runtime. And to make it a bit more complicated, a role could define a set of permissions that could also change at runtime.

Depending on the complexity of the authentication rules that your application must support, you would use one or another approach to authorization. Let's discuss some of them, which, hopefully, will inspire you and give you ideas about how to implement an authorization mechanism suitable for your application.

Coding authorization logic in UI components

The first approach we will discuss is including the authorization logic in the UI components themselves. This is what we have done in the example application, where we show a `PrivateComponent` if the user is authenticated or a `PublicComponent` if they are not. You can extrapolate this and use it with, for example, roles. Suppose there were two roles: *employee* and *admin*. You have to show a hypothetical `AdminComponent` to users with the role admin and an `EmployeeComponent` to users with the *employee* role. You can easily code a method that returns the right component according to the role as follows:

```
private Optional<Component> getComponent(User user) {

    if (user.getRole().equals(Role.Admin)) {
        return new AdminComponent();

    } else if (user.getRole().equals(Role.Employee)) {
        return new EmployeeComponent();
    }

    return Optional.empty();
}
```

If a new `Role` appears in future, you can simply add another `if` clause to cover the case.

What if there's no need for a completely new UI component for a role? For example, let's say the `EmployeeComponent` must show a *delete* button only for users with the *employee* role, and so not for users with the *trainee* role. The easier solution is to code this logic inside the `EmployeeComponent` class itself, using something like the following:

```
public class EmployeeComponent extends Composite {
    public EmployeeComponent() {
        . . .

        User user = AuthService.getCurrentUser();

        if (user.getRole().equals(Role.Employee)) {
            Button delete = new Button();
            someLayout.addComponent(delete);
        }
        . . .
    }
}
```

A good thing about this approach is that you can follow the code to understand what's visible and what's not. However, you might end up with authorization code all over the source code. Well, at least over the UI-related classes. This is, however, a valid approach and you should at least consider it.

A disadvantage of this way of implementing authorization is that it couples UI code with authorization code. This makes it a bit more difficult for software reuse. The preceding class, for example, cannot be used in a different application without carrying the `AuthService` class. Fortunately, we can easily decouple this class from the authentication stuff. The key is the *principle of least privilege*.

The principle of least privilege states that a software entity should have access to the least or minimum amount of data it requires to perform its function. Can you see how the `EmployeeComponent` class violates this principle? All the class needs to know is whether to show the `delete` button or not. It doesn't really care about roles and authentication logic. We are passing way too much information to it. What's the minimal amount of information this class needs to fulfill its requirements? A simple Boolean telling it whether to show the `delete` button or not. That's it. A possible implementation can include a parameter in the constructor for this purpose. Here's an example:

```
public class EmployeeComponent extends Composite {
    public EmployeeComponent(boolean showDeleteButton) {
        . . .
```

```
    if (showDeleteButton) {
        Button delete = new Button();
        someLayout.addComponent(delete);
        ...
    }
    ...
    }
}
```

We just removed the coupling between this class and the authentication logic. However, we moved the authentication logic somewhere else. Now the client of the EmployeeComponent class must configure it depending on the authorization rules. It's not such a bad thing considering that such a client is already coupled to the AuthService class, right? Take a look at the new implementation:

```
private Optional<Component> getComponent(User user) {

    if (user.getRole().equals(Role.Admin)) {
        return new AdminComponent();

    } else if (user.getRole().equals(Role.Employee)) {
        return new EmployeeComponent(true);

    } else if (user.getRole().equals(Role.Trainee)) {
        return new EmployeeComponent(false);
    }

    return Optional.empty();
}
```

 The Optional class serves as a container for a value that may or may not be null (we are not talking about a Vaadin Container here; the Container interface was removed in Vaadin Framework 8.0). Optional helps to decrease the number of null checks in your code. Instead of returning a null value from a method, you can return an Optional, which is empty when the enclosing value is null. This way, the client of the method knows that the returned value might be null. Bear in mind that the original purpose of the Optional class is to serve as an *optional return value*. Avoid using Optional in method parameters.

The main takeaway of this discussion is to keep in mind that you can provide configuration options for your UI components. Don't just unnecessarily couple them with authentication classes. Provide parameters in the constructors, setters, or even configuration classes if the complexity requires it in order to tell the UI component how it should look and behave.

Coding authorization using request data

Let's study a strategy to implement authorization outside UI components. Web frameworks can be classified as:

- Component-based frameworks
- Request/response-based frameworks

Vaadin Framework is a component-based framework. It abstracts away the concept of request and response. You don't have to think much about it when developing a Vaadin application, and that's one of the key features of the framework. Thanks to its ability to allow developers to implement a web application by directly using the Java programming language, developers can use any object-oriented technique to implement features such as authorization. In fact, in the previous section, we explored how to do so using simple Java `if` statements.

Request/response based frameworks, on the other hand, usually make it a bit harder to use the approach we discussed in the previous section (coding the authorization logic directly in the UI component), in part because the UI layer runs in the client side. Coding authentication rules in the client side is a no-go. How do request/response based frameworks implement authorization? Typically, these frameworks include a *front controller*, a software entity that processes all the requests and decides which portion of your code should be invoked. It's then easy to add a *filter* to secure the requested resources according to a set of rules. In short, authorization is implemented with a combination of server-side code (which decides what to show in the browser) and a filter securing URLs according to authorization rules.

Can we use something similar with Vaadin? Let's explore the capabilities of Vaadin regarding *request information* to see how we can take advantage of it in order to design an authentication mechanism that is completely decoupled from the actual UI components.

Getting request information

When we talk about a *request* made to a web application, we are talking about an HTTP request that a client, typically, a browser, makes to the web server. The server takes the *context path* and routes the request to the appropriate web application (for example, a Vaadin application). An important part of the HTTP request is the URL used to access the application and its resources. The following screenshot shows the most important parts of a URL:

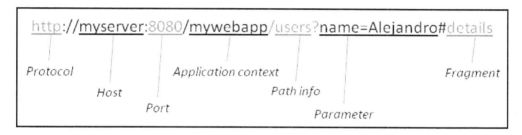

With Vaadin Framework you can get access to all these parts. For example, in order to get the *path info* part of the URL, you can call:

```
String pathInfo = VaadinRequest.getCurrent().getPathInfo();
assert(pathInfo.equals("users"));
```

To get a *parameter* value, you can call:

```
String name = VaadinRequest.getCurrent().getParameter("name");
assert(name.equals("Alejandro"));
```

Routing requests to a UI component

Using the *path info* part and *parameters*, you can already implement a mechanism that *routes* a request to a specific component, similarly to what a front controller does in a request/response-based framework. For example:

```
public class FrontController {
    public static void route(VaadinRequest request,
        SingleComponentContainer container) {

        String path = request.getPathInfo();

        if ("users".equals(path)) {
            container.setContent(new UsersComponent());
```

```
        } else if ("orders".equals(path)) {
            container.setContent(new OrdersComponent());

        } else { ... }
    }
}
```

And the corresponding UI implementation could look like this:

```
public class VaadinUI extends UI {
    @Override
    protected void init(VaadinRequest request) {
        FrontController.route(request, this);
    }
}
```

The FrontController class can invoke any authorization logic in order to decide whether the current user can see a UI component or not before routing the request to a UI component. For example:

```
public class FrontController {
    public static void route(VaadinRequest request,
        SingleComponentContainer container) {
        String path = request.getPathInfo();

        if (!AuthService.userCanAccess(path)) {
            container.setContent(new ErrorComponent(
                "Access denied."));
            return;
        }

        ...

    }
}
```

The AuthService.userCanAccess method can be implemented in various ways:

1. A set of if/else statements checking each path/role combination
2. A check on a Java Map where each key is a path and each value is a Set of the allowed roles for that path
3. A check with an external resource (such as an SQL database, web service, or properties file)
4. An algorithm combining the previous alternatives

Implementing each of these solutions would take too much space in the book, and it's also more related to Java than Vaadin itself, so I'll let you decide how to implement this method.

Coding authorization with the help of a Navigator

You might have heard about the `Navigator` class in Vaadin Framework. In short, the `Navigator` class allows you to pair URI fragments with UI components. When the fragment part changes in the browser, the associated UI component is rendered. It also allows you to programmatically *navigate* to a specific UI component by specifying its associated fragment. For example:

```
public class VaadinUI extends UI {
    @Override
    protected void init(VaadinRequest vaadinRequest) {
        Navigator navigator = new Navigator(this, this);
        navigator.addView("view1", new View1());
        navigator.addView("view2", new View2());
    }
}
```

When you create a `Navigator`, you specify the `UI` to which the `Navigator` is attached and a `ComponentContainer` (such as `VerticalLayout`, for example), whose content will be replaced when the view is made visible (when changing the fragment in the browser, for example). You associate *view names* to UI components by using the `addView` method. In the previous example, we passed instances of the UI components (using the `new` keyword). The `Navigator` class will use these instances throughout the session, so the state of each view is maintained even after navigating away from a view. You can let the `Navigator` class create a new instance of the UI component each time the view is requested by using the overloaded `addView(String, Class<? extends View>)` method. Here's an example:

```
navigator.addView("view1", View1.class);
```

The UI components you can add to a `Navigator` must implement the `View` interface, as shown in the following class:

```
public class View1 extends Composite implements View {
    public View1() {
        setContent(new Label("View 1"));
    }
}
```

Since Vaadin Framework 8.0, the `View` interface includes a Java
8 *default* `enter` method so you don't have to implement it. Vaadin
Framework 8.1 includes some additional default methods you can
implement if needed. Take a look at the reference API of
the `View` interface for more
information: `https://vaadin.com/api/8.3.2/com/vaadin/navigat`
`or/View.html`.

But let's get back to the discussion of authorization strategies. The `Navigator` class allows
you to add a `ViewChangeListener`. We can use this listener to introduce authorization
rules and *secure* UI components. For example:

```
public class AuthViewListener implements ViewChangeListener {

    @Override
    public boolean beforeViewChange(ViewChangeEvent event) {
        if (AuthService.userCanAccess(event.getViewName())) {
            return true;
        }

        return false;
    }
}
```

The `beforeViewChange` method must return `true` to allow the view change and `false` to
block it.

 Vaadin Framework 8.0 added support for the *HTML 5 History API*. With it,
you can avoid having *hashbangs* in the URL (that little `!#` sequence).
Vaadin Framework 8.2 added support for the HTML 5 History API with
the `Navigator` class. You can activate this support by annotating
the `UI` implementation with `@PushStateNavigation`.

Summary

In this chapter, we learned how to keep track of authenticated users by using the HTTP
session. We also learned how to implement the *remember me* feature by using cookies in a
secure way. Finally, we discussed authorization strategies, including coding authorization
logic directly in UI components and coding it by using request data.

In the next chapter, you will learn about how to connect to SQL databases using multiple
Java persistence frameworks with Vaadin.

5
Connecting to SQL Databases Using JDBC

Managing information means performing operations such as storing, modifying, removing, sorting, arranging, linking, and matching data in a data store. Database management systems provide the means to perform these operations and relational databases are the most common type of data store used with web applications.

This chapter starts by briefly discussing the fundamental Java technology for persistence, **Java Database Connectivity** (**JDBC**). We will learn how to connect and how to consume data from a relational database using connection pools and SQL queries. We will also describe the concept of a *data repository*, a way of encapsulating persistence implementation details.

We will develop a very simple web UI that lists data from a database. The purpose of the example is to show you the very fundamentals of database connectivity. Chapter 6, *Connecting to SQL Databases Using ORM Frameworks*, will focus on more advanced database operations with basic data binding.

This chapter covers the following topics:

- JDBC technology
- JDBC drivers
- Connection pools
- SQL query execution
- Data repositories

Technical requirements

You will be required to have Java SE Development Kit and Java EE SDK version 8 or later. You also need Maven version 3 or later. A Java IDE with Maven support, such as IntelliJ IDEA, Eclipse, or NetBeans is recommended. Finally, to use the Git repository of this book, you need to install Git.

The code files of this chapter can be found on GitHub:
`https://github.com/PacktPublishing/Data-centric-Applications-with-Vaadin-8/tree/master/chapter-05`

Check out the following video to see the code in action:
`https://goo.gl/7VonXg`

Introduction to JDBC

If you have developed *business applications* with Java, you have most likely used JDBC directly or indirectly(through an object-relational mapping framework) to connect and use relational databases. A *relational database* is a system for storing information in a tabular form; that is, in tables. There are many vendors offering free and commercial **relational database management systems** (**RDBMS**). Two of the most popular open source RDBMS are *PostgreSQL* and *MySQL*, while *Oracle Database* and *Microsoft SQL Server* are well-known options among the commercial ones. These systems understand the **Structured Query Language** (**SQL**), a *declarative language* used to perform tasks such as adding or deleting rows in a table.

> When using a **declarative language**, you specify *what* you want the program to do. In contrast, when using an **imperative language**, such as the Java programming language, you specify *how* to do it.

Before we get started with the actual code, try compiling and running the example application located in the `Data-centric-Applications-with-Vaadin-8/chapter-05` Maven module. Follow these steps:

1. If you haven't done so, import the `Data-centric-Applications-with-Vaadin-8` Maven project into your IDE.

2. Create a *running configuration* for
   the `packt.vaadin.datacentric.chapter05.jdbc.H2Server` class and run
   it. This is your database server. It runs in a separate process in your
   computer. Alternatively, you can run the H2 server with Maven from the
   `chapter-05` directory: `mvn test exec:java -Dexec.mainClass="packt.vaadin.datacentric.chapter05.jdbc.H2Server"`.

3. Create a running configuration for
   the `packt.vaadin.datacentric.chapter05.jdbc.DatabaseInitialization` class and run it. You should see an **initialization succeeded** message in the
   log. This initialization creates a new table (`messages`) in the database, and adds
   some demo rows to it. Alternatively, you can run the initialization application
   with Maven: `mvn exec:java -Dexec.mainClass="packt.vaadin.datacentric.chapter05.jdbc.DatabaseInitialization"`.

4. Create a running configuration for the Jetty Maven Plugin in the
   `chapter-05` module.

5. Point your browser to `http://localhost:8080`. You should see some demo
   data rendered by a Vaadin application.

6. The H2 server we started in step 2 starts also a web application you can use to
   run SQL queries. Let's try it! Point your browser
   to `http://localhost:8082` and connect using the following configuration:

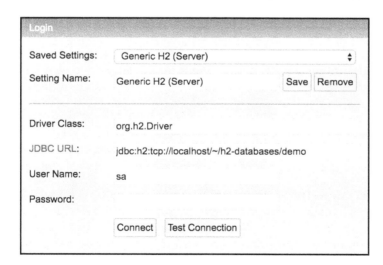

7. Insert a new row into the `messages` table by executing the following SQL statement: `INSERT INTO messages VALUES('Welcome to JDBC!')`.

8. Point your browser to (or reload) the Vaadin application. You should see the new message listed there:

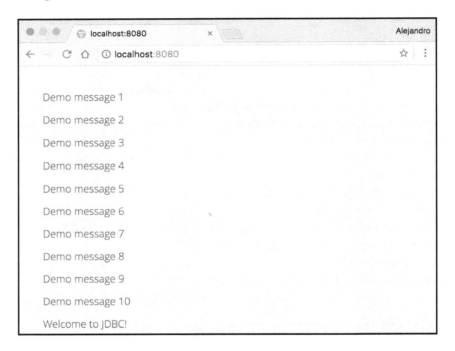

If you want to, you can stop the Vaadin application and the H2 server, and run them again. You should see all the same data as before, including the newly inserted row. Just keep in mind that you need to run the H2 server first!

 If you are curious, the location of the actual H2 database file is `<home-directory>/h2-databases/demo.mv.db`. You can delete this file and run the `DatabaseInitialization` application again if you want to recreate the initial state of the database.

The **Java Database Connectivity (JDBC) API** enables your applications to connect to an RDBMS and make SQL calls to it. Other technologies for SQL persistence are usually implemented on top of the JDBC. Understanding the key aspects of JDBC will make your life easier even if you are planning (or if you are already using) other persistence technologies.

Typically, your application should perform five steps in order to use a database with the JDBC API:

1. Add a **JDBC driver** for your database.
2. Establish a **connection** to the database.
3. Create a **statement** to **execute** an SQL query.
4. Get and process the **result set**.
5. **Close** the connection.

Adding a JDBC driver for your database

Connecting to an RDBMS from a Java application is done through a *JDBC driver*. Most (if not all) database vendors include JDBC drivers for their RDBMS. A JDBC driver, in practice, is just a Java dependency (a JAR) in your project. If, for example, you need to connect your application to a PostgreSQL database, you will need to add the `postgresql-x.x.x.jar` file to your classpath. This, of course, can also be done with Maven. It's through this JDBC driver that your Java application communicates with the RDBMS, and it does so by establishing connections and executing SQL statements to retrieve data.

 We are not covering the details about RDBMS and SQL in this book. These topics are complex enough by themselves to deserve a complete book about them. There are plenty of good bibliographic and online resources you can consult to learn more about these topics.

In this book, we are going to use an H2 database. H2 is a popular open source database engine that doesn't require you to install anything on your computer. All the concepts apply to other RDBMS as well, and we'll include snippets or commented sections in the accompanying code that show the specifics for MySQL and PostgreSQL, in case you want to experiment with these databases by yourself.

Adding a JDBC driver is as simple as including the right dependency in your project. For example, to include the H2 JDBC driver, add the following dependency to your `pom.xml` file:

```
<dependency>
    <groupId>com.h2database</groupId>
    <artifactId>h2</artifactId>
    <version>1.4.196</version>
</dependency>
```

Or if you want to use MySQL or PostgreSQL, add the following dependencies:

```
<dependency>
    <groupId>mysql</groupId>
    <artifactId>mysql-connector-java</artifactId>
    <version>6.0.6</version>
</dependency>

<dependency>
    <groupId>org.postgresql</groupId>
    <artifactId>postgresql</artifactId>
    <version>42.1.4</version>
</dependency>
```

JDBC was designed to support not only relational databases, but also any kind of data source, including file systems or object-oriented systems. Keep this in mind when you need to connect your application to any kind of data source; there might be a JDBC driver for it.

You can, of course, include several JDBC drivers in the same project. The `chapter-05` application includes all of the previous drivers.

In old versions of JDBC, you had to manually load the JDBC driver class using the `Class.forName` method. This is no longer required in JDBC 4.0. Any JDBC 4.0 driver in the classpath is automatically loaded.

Establishing a database connection through a connection pool

One of the most common pitfalls when developing web applications with Vaadin is to forget that what you are developing is actually a web application! Since the API resembles that of desktop-like UI frameworks, it's easy to forget that a Vaadin application is most likely going to be used by several users at the same time. You need to keep the multi user nature of a Vaadin application in mind when establishing connections to a database.

A desktop application you run locally on your machine might be able to work perfectly with a single connection to the database during its execution time (depending on the complexity of the application, of course). This is due to the single-user nature of the application; you know there's only one user per instance. On the other hand, a single instance of a web application is used by many users at the same time. It requires multiple connections to work properly. You don't want to have users *A, B, C..., X* waiting for the connection to be released by greedy user *Z*, right? However, establishing connections is expensive! Opening and closing a connection every time a new user requests the application is not an option, since your app could reach a big number of concurrent users, and hence connections.

This is where a *connection pool* comes in handy. A connection pool is a class that maintains several connections to the database, like a *cache* of connections, if you wish. The connection pool keeps all its connections open so that they can be reused by client classes when they need it. Without a connection pool, any time your app needs to perform a database operation, it has to create a new connection, execute the query, and close the connection. As mentioned previously, this is expensive and wastes resources. Instead, a connection pool creates a set of connections and "lends" them to client classes. Once the connection is used, it's not closed, but returned to the pool and used again.

As you can guess, connection pools are such a well-known pattern that many implementations exist. Let's see how to use one of them, `BoneCP`, a free open source JDBC connection pool implementation.

 Other popular connection pool implementations are *C3P0* and *Apache DBCP*. Moreover, application servers and servlet containers offer the possibility to define pooled data sources (see Java's `DataSource` interface documentation) as part of their configuration. This decouples the data source configuration from your running environment while offering connection pooling mechanisms for free.

First of all, here are the dependencies you need to add:

```xml
<dependency>
    <groupId>com.jolbox</groupId>
    <artifactId>bonecp</artifactId>
    <version>0.8.0.RELEASE</version>
</dependency>
<dependency>
    <groupId>org.slf4j</groupId>
    <artifactId>slf4j-simple</artifactId>
    <version>1.7.25</version>
    <scope>test</scope>
</dependency>
```

BoneCP requires SLF4J, a logging library that offers a *facade* over several logging frameworks. This is needed in order to see logs by BoneCP in the console or web server log.

There should be one instance of the connection pool per instance of the web application. We used a static Java block in the previous chapter to initialize application-level resources. This works in small applications where these resources don't depend on others. In more complex applications, your initialization code might depend on other services (such as *dependency injection*) in order to work, so let's use a more realistic approach this time and use a ServletContextListener to init the connection pool.
A ServletContextListener allows your application to react to events in the *servlet context lifecycle*; in particular, the initialization of a servlet context and its destruction.

As with previous examples, the chapter-05 Vaadin application includes a WebConfig class that defines *everything web*; that is, servlets and event listeners. Besides the VaadinServlet, we can include a ServletContextListener that initializes the database when the servlet context is created (that is when the web application starts... sort of):

```java
@WebListener
public static class JdbcExampleContextListener implements
ServletContextListener {

    @Override
    public void contextInitialized(ServletContextEvent sce) {
        try {
            DatabaseService.init();

        } catch (Exception e) {
            e.printStackTrace();
        }
    }

    @Override
    public void contextDestroyed(ServletContextEvent sce) {
    }
}
```

Thanks to the @WebListener annotation, this class is going to be discovered by the servlet container and registered with the servlet context automatically. Inside the contextInitialized method, we can add the code to initialize the connection pool; in this case, by delegating to the custom DatabaseService class we'll implement next.

The infrastructure code is ready; now it's time for the actual `BoneCp` connection pool. Let's start with the `init` method:

```
public class DatabaseService {

    private static BoneCP pool;

    public static void init() throws SQLException {
        BoneCPConfig config = new BoneCPConfig();
        config.setJdbcUrl("jdbc:h2:tcp://localhost/~/h2-databases/demo");
        config.setUsername("sa");
        config.setPassword("");

        pool = new BoneCP(config);
    }
}
```

This implementation defines a static (only one instance per application) `BoneCP` field, `pool`, the actual connection pool. The `pool` field is initialized in the `init` method, which is called when the application starts (see the `JdbcExampleContextListener` class).

There are three things you need to specify when connecting to a database with JDBC:

- **The connection URL**: With JDBC, a database is represented by a connection URL. JDBC uses this URL to get the information about where and how to connect to the database. In the previous example, we can see that the string contains the name of the database (`h2`), a host (`localhost`), and a database name (`~/h2-databases/demo`).
- **The username**: Databases allow you to define a set of users, roles, and permissions. The username is an identifier that the database can check in order to grant permissions on the data. By default, the H2 database defines the username `sa`.
- **The password**: As you can guess, this is what allows the database engine to run the authentication check. By default, H2 uses an empty password for the default `sa` user.

What if you wanted to use MySQL or PostgreSQL now? you would have to change the String literals in this class, recompile, and redeploy. A much better approach is to externalize this String. One approach is to use the standard Java Properties class to load *key/value* pairs with the connection URL, username, and password. For example, the chapter-05 application includes a datasource.properties file in the /src/main/resources directory:

```
datasource.url=jdbc:h2:tcp://localhost/~/h2-databases/demo
datasource.username=sa
datasource.password=
```

With MySQL databases,
use: datasource.url=jdbc:mysql://localhost/demo
With PostgreSQL databases,
use: datasource.url=jdbc:postgresql://localhost:5432/demo

The DatabaseService class can now use these properties (datasource.*) instead of the *hard-coded* literals:

```java
public class DatabaseService {

    private static String url;
    private static String password;
    private static String username;
    private static BoneCP pool;

    public static void init() throws SQLException, IOException {
        loadProperties();
        createPool();
    }

    private static void loadProperties() throws IOException {
        try (InputStream inputStream =
DatabaseService.class.getClassLoader().getResourceAsStream("datasource.properties")) {
            Properties properties = new Properties();
            properties.load(inputStream);

            url = properties.getProperty("datasource.url");
            username = properties.getProperty("datasource.username");
            password = properties.getProperty("datasource.password");
        }
    }

    private static void createPool() {
        ...
```

```
        config.setJdbcUrl(url);
        config.setUsername(username);
        config.setPassword(password);
        . . .
    }
}
```

The connection properties (`url`, `username`, and `password`) are now static fields in the class populated from the `datasource.properties` file.

A way of making your web application configuration independent of the running environment is to use the operating system's *environment variables*. For example, let's say you define a `MY-WEBAPP-CONF-DIRECTORY` environment variable in your computer, and set its value to `~/my-webapp-conf`. Inside this directory, you can put all the `.properties` files that make up the configuration for example, the `datasource.properties` file. The web application can read the environment variable like this: `String confDirectory = System.getenv("MY-WEBAPP-CONF-DIRECTORY")`, and read any files inside this directory in order to configure the application accordingly. With this technique, each developer in the team can define their own local configuration. Moreover, you can easily configure *test* and *production* environments by defining the environment variable and placing the corresponding configuration files – no need to worry about replacing files when you deploy to these environments besides checking that all configuration properties are in place. Make sure you show good error or warning messages when a property doesn't exist.

Now that we have a connection pool ready, we can get actual connections to the database. Here is how:

```
Connection connection = pool.getConnection();
```

A `Connection` represents a session with the database. This interface contains a number of methods to get information about the capabilities of the database and the state of the connection, but the most important part allows you to create `Statements` objects.

 Connection pool implementations offer good configurations for development or testing environments. This is most likely not optimal for a production environment. Consult the documentation of the implementation, and tune the configuration accordingly when deploying to production environments.

Creating a statement and executing an SQL query

A `Statement` object is used to invoke SQL statements in the database. The following snippet of code shows how to retrieve a `Connection` object from the connection pool. This object is used to create a new `Statement`, which, in turn, is used to execute an SQL statement:

```
try (Connection connection = pool.getConnection()) {
    Statement statement = connection.createStatement();
    ResultSet resultSet = statement.execute("SELECT content FROM
messages");
}
```

 In this chapter, we are using the `Statement` interface and its `createStatement` counterpart method. In more critical applications, you should use the `PreparedStatement` interface and the `prepareStatement` method in order to increase performance and prevent SQL injection attacks.

Getting and processing a result set

As you can see, the `execute` method of the `Statement` class returns a `ResultSet` object. A `ResultSet` object represents data from the database. It works like a cursor pointing to the rows in the data. First, the cursor is placed before the first row. You can use the `next` method to iterate through the rows as follows:

```
while (resultSet.next()) {
    String content = resultSet.getString("content");
}
```

In the previous example, we are using the `getString` method to get the value that corresponds to the `content` column. There are methods for various data types: for example, the `getInt` method returns the value in the specified column as a Java `int`.

Closing a database connection

When using a connection pool, the pool implementation takes care of closing the JDBC connections. Depending on the specific implementation, you might have to invoke this process. Usually, you want the pool to be active during the lifetime of your web application. Remember the `ServletContextListener` implementation we used to initialize the connection pool? Well, we can use it to shut the pool down. All we need to do is to implement the `contextDestroyed` method:

```
@WebListener
public static class JdbcExampleContextListener implements
ServletContextListener {
    ...

    @Override
    public void contextDestroyed(ServletContextEvent sce) {
        DatabaseService.shutdown();
    }
}
```

Finally, the `shutdown` method is implemented as follows:

```
public class DatabaseService {
    ...
    public static void shutdown() {
        pool.shutdown();
    }
}
```

Now, it's a good time for you to play with the chapter-05 demo application again. Have a close look at the DatabaseService class and how it is used in the VaadinUI class. The findAllMessages method is pretty interesting in particular, as it acts as the main communication point between the Vaadin application and the UI:

```java
package packt.vaadin.datacentric.chapter05.jdbc;

import com.jolbox.bonecp.BoneCP;
import com.jolbox.bonecp.BoneCPConfig;

import java.io.IOException;
import java.io.InputStream;
import java.sql.Connection;
import java.sql.ResultSet;
import java.sql.SQLException;
import java.sql.Statement;
import java.util.ArrayList;
import java.util.List;
import java.util.Properties;

/**
 * @author Alejandro Duarte
 */
public class DatabaseService {

    private static final String SELECT_SQL = "SELECT content FROM messages";
    private static final String CONTENT_COLUMN = "content";
    . . .

    public static List<String> findAllMessages() throws SQLException {
        try (Connection connection = pool.getConnection()) {
            Statement statement = connection.createStatement();
            ResultSet resultSet = statement.executeQuery(SELECT_SQL);

            List<String> messages = new ArrayList<>();
            while (resultSet.next()) {
                messages.add(resultSet.getString(CONTENT_COLUMN));
            }

            return messages;
        }
    }
    . . .

}
```

See how the SQL queries are defined in String constants. Can you think of a better way of doing this? In a more complex application, you might end up having hundreds of SQL queries. A better practice in these scenarios is to externalize the SQL code. Properties files might help, but defining SQL queries in a single line could be a challenge, to say the least. A better approach is XML, a format that allows you to use multiple lines to define values. We'll see how MyBatis promotes this approach in Chapter 6, *Connecting to SQL Databases Using ORM Frameworks*.

Another interesting detail in the findAllMessages method is the return type. Why not return a ResultSet object? We do this to avoid coupling the presentation layer with persistence implementation details. This is what we are going to explore in the following section.

You might have noticed that the findAllMessages method can throw an SQLException. This makes clients of this method aware of implementation details at some level. Although the name of the exception class implies SQL is being used, according to the API documentation, an SQLException is *"an exception that provides information on a database access error or other errors"*. This exception is used even in drivers for *NoSQL* databases.

Implementing data repositories

A *repository*, for the purposes of this book, is a class that includes all or some of the **CRUD** operations (**Create, Read, Update, and Delete**). Repositories encapsulate persistence details in an application. A repository holds the means to the domain model (or entities).

More precisely, a domain model includes not only data, but also behavior. Another term used widely is **data transfer object** (**DTO**). Although the original definition of DTO was intended to describe a way to transport data between processes, many architectures (inaccurately) define DTO as an object that carries data between software components in the same process. To complicate things even more, there are *value objects* (objects that are equal if their properties are equal), and *entities* (objects that are equal based on their identity, which can be defined by a single property). When documenting and designing your software, spend some time investigating the terms, and try to choose the one that best matches your design.

Defining a domain model

Let's study this with an example. Suppose you are implementing a simple e-commerce application. You are in charge of the *orders module,* and have to provide access to the data related to this module through a web UI. After reading the specification, you designed a simple domain model formed by the following classes:

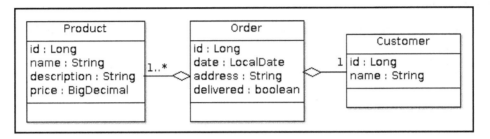

This is pretty straightforward: an `Order` has one or more `Product` objects and one `Customer`. You want to use the hypothetical *Technology X* to persist data (it doesn't matter which one for this example), and you want your Vaadin `UI` implementation to be able to directly use the domain class; however, you don't want to couple your UI implementation with Technology X. Moreover, you have to expose orders and product data through a web service for an external accounting system. You decided, then, to implement three repositories, one for each domain class: `ProductRepository`, `OrderRepository`, and `CustomerRepository`.

Implementing repositories and services

At this point, you started implementing the Vaadin UI, and had a clear understanding of the methods that the repositories should expose. You then implemented these methods in the respective repository classes:

ProductRepository	OrderRepository	CustomerRepository
persistence : TechnologyX	persistence : TechnologyX	persistence : TechnologyX
findAll() : List<Product> findByOderId(Long) : List<Poduct>	getByCustomerId(Long) : Customer	getById(Long) : Customer

Let's take a closer look at the methods in the repository classes. As you can see, all method names start with `find` or `get`. This is a well-known convention in the industry, and it's used by libraries such as **Spring Data** or **Apache DeltaSpike**. Methods starting with `find` return a collection of objects, while methods starting with `get` return single, ready-to-use values (such as a domain instance, or one of its properties).

Notice how each repository has a private `persistence` field that represents the entry point to use Technology X, we will see concrete examples of this later in this chapter. If, for some reason, you had to change the persistence technology to something else, client classes wouldn't be affected. Moreover, you can use different persistence technologies for different repositories without having client classes to deal with different APIs. The following code will give you a clear idea of how these repositories can be implemented:

```
public class OrderRepository {

    private TechnologyX persistence = ...

    public List<Product> findAll() {
        ... use Technology X through the persistence instance to fetch the
data ...
        ... convert the data to a List ...
        return list;
    }
    ...
}
```

All the implementation details regarding how to get the data are encapsulated in the repository class. Now, let's move on and see how this can be used from a Vaadin application.

While doing *pair programming,* your colleague suggested you should use service classes to abstract away the concept of *repository* from the Vaadin UI. She argued that there should be one `service` class for each repository: `ProductService`, `OrderService`, and `CustomerService`. It seemed like a good idea to you too; however, she immediately noticed that the service classes would be simple *facades* for their repository counterparts, and wouldn't include any extra logic. You pointed out that the application had to expose data through a web service consumed by the accounting system, and that the service classes might be used for that. After you and your colleague investigated the precise data the web service had to expose, you both decided to *Fight for Simplicity,* and not to implement one `service` class per `repository` class.

Instead, the Vaadin UI would be allowed to have references to the repository classes. You also decided to implement a separate `AccountingWebService` class to expose the data for the accounting system, so that you could know and control what this system is "seeing" in the future. As with the Vaadin UI classes, the web service implementation would use the repository classes to fetch data.

 The previous hypothetical example doesn't imply that you shouldn't enforce a repository/service pairing kind of design in your projects. Always stop and think before making this kind of decision. The situation in the example shows how the developers considered alternatives, investigated the requirements more deeply, and then took an informed decision. Keep the developers, who will maintain your code in the future in mind. Keep your legacy in mind.

The active record pattern

There are many architectural patterns that may or may not help in your projects; in particular, regarding domain models and persistence. You might want to have a look at the *active record pattern*. An active record class encapsulates not only the data, but also its persistence operations. For example, the `Order` class of the previous example would look like the following:

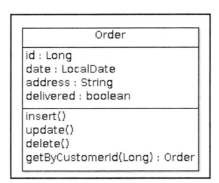

Notice how the CRUD operations are implemented in the domain class alongside with the methods previously implemented in the `repository` class. Although being an alternative to keep in mind, we won't further cover or use the active record pattern in this book.

Summary

This chapter served as the fundamentals of database connectivity with Java. We learned concepts such as JDBC drivers (that allow applications to connect to specific relational database engines) and connection pools (to better use connection resources). We learned how to use a `ContextServletListener` to initialize connection pools or database-related services. We saw an example of a simple domain model, and how repository classes allow us to encapsulate access to data represented in this model.

In the next chapter, we are going to learn about several persistence technologies, and how to integrate them with the Vaadin Framework.

6
Connecting to SQL Databases Using ORM Frameworks

The **Vaadin Framework** is a *web framework—a* library, if you wish, that helps with *web development*. You, as a developer, have the opportunity to integrate it with any other Java technology, and in particular, with any persistence technology. Since the most popular technology for persisting data is SQL, this chapter is dedicated to exploring several alternatives to connecting to SQL databases from Vaadin applications.

We will start by studying the concept of *object-relational mapping*, a technique that allows developers to use an object-oriented programming language to consume and manipulate data in an otherwise incompatible system. We'll then move on to explore three of the most popular Java frameworks used to connect to SQL databases: *JPA, MyBatis*, and *jOOQ*. These technologies are widely used in the industry, and it's important that you understand at least the philosophy and fundamentals of each one in order to select the best options for your projects.

Throughout the sections in this chapter, we will develop very simple web UIs that list data from a database (using the `Grid` class), and present a simple form to add data to it. The purpose of the examples is to show you the very fundamentals of data binding with Vaadin. The next chapter will focus on more advanced data binding to develop sophisticated **CRUD (Create, Read, Update, and Delete)** user interfaces.

This chapter covers the following topics:

- **Object-relational mapping (ORM)** frameworks
- **Java Persistence API (JPA)**
- MyBatis
- **Java Object Oriented Querying (jOOQ)**

Technical requirements

You will be required to have Java SE Development Kit and Java EE SDK version 8 or later. You also need Maven version 3 or later. A Java IDE with Maven support, such as IntelliJ IDEA, Eclipse, or NetBeans is recommended. Finally, to use the Git repository of this book, you need to install Git.

The code files of this chapter can be found on GitHub:
`https://github.com/PacktPublishing/Data-centric-Applications-with-Vaadin-8/tree/master/chapter-06`

Check out the following video to see the code in action:
`https://goo.gl/p1CGkr`

Using object-relational mapping frameworks

In a relational database, data is represented as *tables*. In a Java program, data is represented as *objects*. For example, if you have data related to customers, you can store this data in a `customers` table. Similarly, you can store this data in objects which are instances of the `Customer` class. *Object-relational mapping* frameworks allow you to convert the data between these two systems.

We already learned how to fetch data via JDBC and the `ResultSet` interface in the previous chapter. You could take an instance of this interface, iterate over the rows, and manually set the fields of a Java class such as `Customer`. When you do so, you are doing the job of an ORM framework. Why reinvent the wheel? The Java ecosystem offers several options to fix the *object-relational impedance mismatch*. In the following sections, we'll examine three of the most popular alternatives to solve this impedance mismatch.

 The Object Oriented paradigm is based on software engineering principles, while the Relational paradigm is based on mathematical principles. The *object-relational impedance mismatch* refers to the incompatibility between these two paradigms.

The examples developed in the following sections use the H2 database instance we initialized during the introduction to JDBC in the previous chapter. Make sure that the H2 server is running and that the `messages` table exists (see the `packt.vaadin.datacentric.chapter05.jdbc.DatabaseInitialization` class for details). You can use any other database if you want. If so, make sure your database server is running, create the `messages` table, and configure your application to point to your new database.

Connecting to SQL databases using JPA

The first thing you need to know about the JPA is that it is a specification, not an implementation. There are several implementations, *Hibernate* and *EclipseLink* arguably being the most popular ones. In this book, we'll use Hibernate. The other things you need to learn about JPA are better learned by coding! Let's see how to create a simple Vaadin application that shows a `Grid` with the messages in the database.

What do you think is the first thing you need to do to start using JPA, or more specifically, Hibernate? It's, of course, adding the dependencies. Create a Vaadin project and add the following dependencies to your `pom.xml` file:

```
<dependency>
    <groupId>org.hibernate</groupId>
    <artifactId>hibernate-core</artifactId>
    <version>5.2.10.Final</version>
</dependency>
```

You can find all the code developed in this section in the `Data-centric-Applications-with-Vaadin-8/chapter-06/jpa-example` **Maven** project.

Defining a persistence unit

So, JPA is ready in the classpath. What could be the next logical step? It makes sense to define a connection to the database next. The simplest way of doing this is by creating a `persistence.xml` file. JPA will automatically read this file in the `META-INF` directory in your classpath. In a Maven project, the location is `resources/META-INF/persistence.xml`. Inside this file, you can define one or more *persistence units* (database connections) and its connection properties. The following is an example of a minimal `persistence.xml` file you can use to connect to the H2 database:

```
<persistence xmlns="http://java.sun.com/xml/ns/persistence"
             xmlns:xsi="http://www.w3.org/2001/XMLSchema-instance"
             xsi:schemaLocation="http://java.sun.com/xml/ns/persistence
             http://java.sun.com/xml/ns/persistence/persistence_2_0.xsd"
             version="2.0">
    <persistence-unit name="jpa-example-pu">
      <properties>
        <property name="javax.persistence.jdbc.url"
        value="jdbc:h2:tcp://localhost/~/h2-databases/demo" />
        <property name="javax.persistence.jdbc.user" value="sa" />
```

```
                    <property name="javax.persistence.jdbc.password" value="" />
                </properties>
            </persistence-unit>
        </persistence>
```

Since you can define multiple persistence units (when your application needs to connect to multiple databases, for example), each persistence unit must have a name that identifies it. We have used `jpa-example-pu` for ours. Notice how we used the same connection properties (URL, user, password) we used previously with plain JDBC.

Creating an EntityManagerFactory

We have *defined* a connection through a persistence unit, but the application is not actually *using* it yet. The way applications make use of JPA is through the `EntityManagerFactory`. You can think of the `EntityManagerFactory` as the *entry point to JPA*. An `EntityManagerFactory` allows you to interact with a specific persistence unit. It's almost, but not precisely, like the connection pool, if you like.

 JPA implementations, like Hibernate or EclipseLink, offer built-in connection pooling mechanisms which are handled internally. You can usually adjust the pool configuration by using additional properties in the persistence unit definition. Consult the documentation of the JPA implementation you use for more details.

In our case, there's only one persistence unit, `jpa-example-pu`, so it makes sense to have only one `EntityManagerFactory` instance per instance of the application. As with plain JDBC, we can use `ServletContextListener` to create the `EntityManagerFactory`, but once again, let's delegate this to a different class to encapsulate JPA-related stuff:

```
public class JPAService {

    private static EntityManagerFactory factory;

    public static void init() {
        if (factory == null) {
            factory = Persistence.createEntityManagerFactory("jpa-
                example-pu");
        }
    }

    public static void close() {
        factory.close();
    }
```

```
    public static EntityManagerFactory getFactory() {
        return factory;
    }
}
```

We have defined the `init` and `close` methods to initialize and close
the `EntityManagerFactory`, respectively. These methods can be used in
a `ServletContextListener`:

```
@WebListener
public class JpaExampleContextListener implements ServletContextListener {

    @Override
    public void contextInitialized(ServletContextEvent sce) {
        JPAService.init();
    }

    @Override
    public void contextDestroyed(ServletContextEvent sce) {
        JPAService.close();
    }
}
```

The `JPAService` method also exposes
the `EntityManagerFactory` instance though the `getFactory` method. This is where
things start to get more functional. With JPA, you use an `EntityManagerFactory` to
create `EntityManager` instances. Think of an `EntityManager` as a *working unit*, a concrete
interaction you need to perform with the database, for example, saving data or reading it.
Some class could use the `JPAService.getFactory` method to, for example, get all the
messages from the database. Omitting the code that actually queries the database and
exception handling, the following is the *general infrastructure* code to interact with the
database with JPA:

```
EntityManager entityManager =
JPAService.getFactory().createEntityManager();
entityManager.getTransaction().begin();

... run queries ...

entityManager.getTransaction().commit();
entityManager.close();
```

This code gets the `EntityManagerFactory` to create a new `EntityManager`. With it, a new database transaction can be started. After this, you can put the code that actually runs queries against the database, but before we unveil the ... `run queries` ... code, we need to implement an important class we are missing.

Implementing Entity classes

JPA is an ORM framework. It *maps* SQL tables to Java objects. We already have the SQL table, `messages`, but what about the Java counterpart? We need to define a `Message` class. If you had a look at the code for the JDBC section, you probably saw the SQL code to create the messages table. If not, here it is:

```
CREATE TABLE messages(id BIGINT auto_increment, content VARCHAR(255))
```

We want that table to be represented on the Java side as:

```
public class Message {

    private Long id;
    private String content;

    ... getters and setters ...
}
```

This class is going to be what JPA calls an Entity class, a **POJO** class (**Plain Old Java Object**) that is annotated to match an SQL table. You can use annotations to *tell* JPA how to *map* the objects to the tables. The code speaks by itself:

```
@Entity
@Table(name = "messages")
public class Message {

    @Id
    private Long id;

    private String content;

    ... getters and setters ...
}
```

We are using the `@Entity` annotation to mark the class as an Entity. `@Table` tells JPA which SQL table to map to. `@Id` marks the property that corresponds to the primary key in the SQL table. How about the `auto_increment` definition for the `id` column in the messages table? We don't want to worry about *counting* IDs to keep track of which value to use next, right? We can tell JPA that this column is generated by the database as follows:

```
@Id
@GeneratedValue(strategy = GenerationType.IDENTITY)
private Long id;
```

Depending on your database, you may want to use a different strategy. For example, with PostgreSQL, you would most likely use `GenerationType.SEQUENCE` instead.

The `id` column in the messages table defines the *identity* of a row. It has to be the same as its Java counterpart. We can do this by overriding the `equals` method, and because of the `Object.hashCode` method contract, we also need to override the `hashCode` method:

```
public class Message {
    ...

    @Override
    public boolean equals(Object o) {
        if (this == o) return true;
        if (o == null || getClass() != o.getClass()) return false;

        Message message = (Message) o;

        return id != null ? id.equals(message.id) : message.id == null;
    }

    @Override
    public int hashCode() {
        return id != null ? id.hashCode() : 0;
    }

    ...
}
```

According to the JavaDocs for the `Object.equals` method: "...it is generally necessary to override the `hashCode` method whenever this method is overridden, so as to maintain the general contract for the `hashCode` method, which states that equal objects must have equal hash codes". Most IDEs include a feature to generate this code for you.

Executing queries

The connection properties are ready, the `EntityManagerFactory` is ready, and the Entity class is ready. Time to unveil the . . . `run queries` . . . part:

```
Query query = entityManager.createQuery("select m from Message m");
List<Message> messages = query.getResultList();
```

At first, you might think `select m from Message m` is SQL code. But it's not! First of all, there's no `Messages` table in the database (it's `messages`). Second of all, this query is a **Java Persistence Query Language (JPQL)** query.

 JPQL is a platform-independent language similar to SQL. JPA converts JPQL queries to corresponding SQL queries that can be sent to the database. There's not enough space in this chapter to cover all the features of JPQL. There are plenty of resources online about it if you want to learn more.

The previous code looks exactly like something you would encapsulate in a repository class. Let's do so and implement a `MessageRepository` class as follows:

```
public class MessageRepository {

    public static List<Message> findAll() {
        EntityManager entityManager = null;
        try {
            entityManager =
            JPAService.getFactory().createEntityManager();
            entityManager.getTransaction().begin();

            Query query = entityManager.createQuery("select m from
            Message m");
            List<Message> messages = query.getResultList();

            entityManager.getTransaction().commit();
            return messages;
```

```
        } finally {
            if (entityManager != null) {
                entityManager.close();
            }
        }
    }

}
```

There's a lot of boilerplate code. Repository classes like to have many methods, and most of them will need the same kind of infrastructure code to run a single query. Fortunately, we can use some Java constructs to encapsulate the logic for creating an EntityManager, opening and closing a transaction, and closing the EntityManager. The JPAService class looks like the perfect candidate for this:

```
public class JPAService {
    ...

    public static <T> T runInTransaction(Function<EntityManager, T>
        function) {
        EntityManager entityManager = null;

        try {
            entityManager =
            JPAService.getFactory().createEntityManager();
            entityManager.getTransaction().begin();

            T result = function.apply(entityManager);

            entityManager.getTransaction().commit();
            return result;

        } finally {
            if (entityManager != null) {
                entityManager.close();
            }
        }
    }

}
```

The `runInTransaction` method is a generic method that uses a Java `Function` which delegates the actual query logic to clients. Thanks to Java lambda expressions, we can clean up the code in the `MessagesService` class as follows:

```
public class MessageRepository {

    public static List<Message> findAll() {
        return JPAService.runInTransaction(em ->
            em.createQuery("select m from Message m").getResultList()
        );
    }
}
```

We can also add a method to save new messages. With JPA, this is pretty simple:

```
public class MessageRepository {
    ...

    public static void save(Message message) {
        JPAService.runInTransaction(em -> {
            em.persist(message);
            return null;
        });
    }
}
```

Notice how the `EntityManager.persist` method directly accepts an instance of the `Message` Entity class.

 Note that the configuration and code examples in this chapter are valid in the context of web applications that use the Servlet specification only. When using the full Jakarta EE (previously Java EE) specification or Spring Framework, the configuration and code have subtle variations and practices. For example, you should use JNDI discoverable data sources configured in the server instead of specifying usernames and passwords for database connections with Jakarta EE. Also, transaction boundaries can be automatically managed with Jakarta EE and Spring Framework, which means that you don't need to implement and use the `runInTransaction` method.

Implementing a Vaadin UI to list and save Entities

How can we use this from a Vaadin UI? Not a mystery at all, right? Just use Vaadin components and call the `MessageRepository` class when needed. Let's see it in action! Start by implementing a basic UI that shows a `Grid`, a `TextField`, and a `Button`, something like the following:

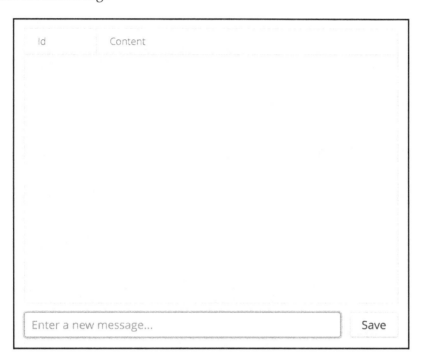

Feel free to implement a different layout for it. The following is the implementation corresponding to the previous screenshot:

```
public class VaadinUI extends UI {

    private Grid<Message> grid;
    private TextField textField;
    private Button button;

    @Override
    protected void init(VaadinRequest request) {
        initLayout();
        initBehavior();
    }
```

```
        private void initLayout() {
            grid = new Grid<>(Message.class);
            grid.setSizeFull();
            grid.getColumn("id").setWidth(100);

            textField = new TextField();
            textField.setPlaceholder("Enter a new message...");
            textField.setSizeFull();

            button = new Button("Save");

            HorizontalLayout formLayout = new HorizontalLayout(textField,
    button);
            formLayout.setWidth("100%");
            formLayout.setExpandRatio(textField, 1);

            VerticalLayout layout = new VerticalLayout(grid, formLayout);
            layout.setWidth("600px");
            setContent(layout);
        }

        private void initBehavior() {
            // not yet implemented! Stay tuned!
        }
    }
```

The previous implementation shows a good practice: separating the code that builds up the UI from the code that adds behavior to it. The behavior, in this case, means adding a `ClickListener` that saves the message in the `TextField` and showing messages from the database in the grid. The following completes the implementation of the behavior for the UI:

```
    public class VaadinUI extends UI {
        ...

        private void initBehavior() {
            button.addClickListener(e -> saveCurrentMessage());
            update();
        }

        private void saveCurrentMessage() {
            Message message = new Message();
            message.setContent(textField.getValue());
            MessageRepository.save(message);

            update();
            grid.select(message);
```

```
        grid.scrollToEnd();
    }

    private void update() {
        grid.setItems(MessageRepository.findAll());
        textField.clear();
        textField.focus();
    }
}
```

We are directly using the `MessageRepository` class to invoke persistence-related logic. Notice how the *data binding* is done in the `saveCurrentMessage` method. This binding goes in only one direction: from the UI to the Entity. This is the most basic form of data binding you can use with Vaadin. In the case of the `Grid`, the data binding goes in the other direction: from the Entities to the UI. We'll see more advanced data binding techniques in the next chapter.

 When should you use JPA? In general, JPA is good for RDBMS portability. JPA is widely used in the industry and there are many tools and resources available for it. JPA is an official Java specification with several vendors offering implementations (such as Hibernate and EclipseLink). JPA is not the only official Java specification for persistence. **Java Data Objects (JDO)** is another Java specification you may want to, at least, consider.

Connecting to SQL databases using MyBatis

MyBatis is a persistence framework that maps SQL to Java objects. The MyBatis learning curve is flatter than JPA's and leverages on SQL, which makes it a good match if you have good knowledge about SQL or have many complex SQL queries you want to reuse.

As usual, you first need to add the dependency. Here is how to do it with Maven:

```
<dependency>
    <groupId>org.mybatis</groupId>
    <artifactId>mybatis</artifactId>
    <version>3.4.5</version>
</dependency>
```

You can find the full implementation of the example developed in this section in the `Data-centric-Applications-with-Vaadin-8/chapter-06/mybatis-example` Maven project.

Defining a database connection

With MyBatis, you can define a database connection using a Java API or a configuration XML file. The easiest way is to put an XML file in the classpath (the `resources` directory, when using Maven). The following is an example of such a configuration file:

```xml
<?xml version="1.0" encoding="UTF-8" ?>
<!DOCTYPE configuration
PUBLIC "-//mybatis.org//DTD Config 3.0//EN"
        "http://mybatis.org/dtd/mybatis-3-config.dtd">
<configuration>
    <environments default="development">
        <environment id="development">
            <transactionManager type="JDBC"/>
            <dataSource type="POOLED">
                <property name="driver" value="org.h2.Driver"/>
                <property name="url"
                 value="jdbc:h2:tcp://localhost/~/h2-databases/demo"/>
                <property name="username" value="sa"/>
                <property name="password" value=""/>
            </dataSource>
        </environment>
    </environments>
    <mappers>
        <mapper
     class="packt.vaadin.datacentric.chapter06.mybatis.MessageMapper"/>
    </mappers>
</configuration>
```

You can use any name for this file. The example for this section uses `mybatis-config.xml`.

As you can see, we used the same connection properties we used for JDBC and JPA, but we added a `driver` property. Its value should correspond to the name of JDBC driver which you are going to use for the database connection.

How do we use this file? Once again, we can use a `ServletContextListener` to initialize MyBatis. Moreover, the `ServletContextListener` can delegate to a service class like the following:

```
public class MyBatisService {

    private static SqlSessionFactory sqlSessionFactory;

    public static void init() {
        InputStream inputStream =
MyBatisService.class.getResourceAsStream("/mybatis-config.xml");
        sqlSessionFactory = new
SqlSessionFactoryBuilder().build(inputStream);
    }

    public static SqlSessionFactory getSqlSessionFactory() {
        return sqlSessionFactory;
    }
}
```

The `SqlSessionFactory` class is the *entry point* to MyBatis. The previous class provides the init method that can be called from a `ServletContextListener`, which creates one `SqlSessionFactory` per instance of the application, and exposes it through a getter. This is a pattern similar to the one we previously used with JPA.

Implementing mapper classes

MyBatis uses *mapper classes* (actually, interfaces) to define the methods that will map SQL queries to Java objects. These are almost the equivalent of the repository classes we have developed so far. However, it makes sense to use MyBatis terminology when using it. Also, as we'll see later, we need to add transaction or session management code around the calls to the mapper class, but let's start with the mapper class. If you were observant, the `mybatis-config.xml` file defined a mapper class in the `mappers` section. Go back and have a look at it. The following is the definition of such a mapper:

```
public interface MessageMapper {

    @Select("SELECT id, content FROM messages")
    List<Message> findAll();

    @Insert("INSERT INTO messages(content) VALUES (#{content})")
```

```
@Options(useGeneratedKeys = true, keyProperty = "id")
void save(Message message);

}
```

As you can see, `MessageMapper` is an interface. You don't have to implement this interface; MyBatis will provide the implementation for you at runtime. We have defined two methods: one to return a `List` of Messages, and another to save a `Message`. Notice the `@Select` and `@Insert` annotations. These are used to define the SQL that will run when these methods are called. Also, notice how you can pass values from the arguments to the SQL query. The save method accepts a `Message` instance. In the SQL query defined by the `@Insert` annotation, we use `#{content}` to *pass* the value of the `Message.content` property to the query. You could have passed a `String` with the value too. In that case, you can use the name of the parameter directly. However, we want MyBatis to set the value of the `id` property after the row has been inserted. This value is autogenerated in the database, so we have to use the `@Options` annotation to configure this behavior.

Implementing a service class

As mentioned before, we need to add some transaction and session handling code in order to use mapper classes. This can be done in *service classes*. A service class is simply a class that performs some kind of business logic (in contrast, a mapper class performs persistence-only logic). The following is an example of a class that encapsulates session handling in order to avoid coupling the UI with MyBatis-related logic:

```
public class MessageService {

    public static List<Message> findAll() {
        try (SqlSession session =
          MyBatisService.getSqlSessionFactory().openSession()) {
            MessageMapper mapper =
              session.getMapper(MessageMapper.class);
            return mapper.findAll();
        }
    }

    public static void save(Message message) {
        try (SqlSession session =
MyBatisService.getSqlSessionFactory().openSession()) {
            MessageMapper mapper = session.getMapper(MessageMapper.class);
            mapper.save(message);
            session.commit();
```

```
        }
     }
  }
```

Each persistence unit of work should be enclosed by an active session. Additionally, for insert or updates, we need to commit the transaction to the database.

MyBatis is a powerful and mature framework you should keep in mind when deciding on technologies. There are many other features, such as the possibility to map methods to SQL stored procedures or using XML files (or even the Apache Velocity scripting language) to define the SQL queries, which is useful when the queries require multiple lines or need to be formed dynamically.

Connecting to SQL databases using jOOQ

jOOQ is a persistence framework that allows you to define SQL queries using the Java Programming Language. It has many capabilities and this section, we will only show a few of them.

As always, you can start by adding the required dependencies to start using jOOQ:

```
<dependency>
    <groupId>org.jooq</groupId>
    <artifactId>jooq</artifactId>
    <version>3.9.5</version>
</dependency>
<dependency>
    <groupId>org.jooq</groupId>
    <artifactId>jooq-codegen</artifactId>
    <version>3.9.5</version>
</dependency>
```

You can find all the code developed in this section in the Data-centric-Applications-with-Vaadin-8/chapter-06/jooq-example Maven project.

Defining a database connection

You can use jOOQ with any connection pool you prefer. The example for this section uses the same approach we used with plain JDBC, so the connection properties can be defined in a `datasource.properties` file:

```
datasource.url=jdbc:h2:tcp://localhost/~/h2-databases/demo
datasource.username=sa
datasource.password=
```

At this point, you should be familiar with how to use a `ServletContextListener` to initialize a database connection pool. Let's omit that part (see the section about JDBC for details) and jump directly to more specific topics.

Reverse-engineering the database schema

Let's say you have a database schema to manage books and authors. A possible SQL query for such a database could look like the following:

```
SELECT AUTHOR.FIRST_NAME, AUTHOR.LAST_NAME
FROM AUTHOR
ORDER BY AUTHOR.LAST_NAME ASC
```

jOOQ allows you to write this same SQL query, but in Java:

```
dslContext.select(AUTHOR.FIRST_NAME, AUTHOR.LAST_NAME)
        .from(AUTHOR)
        .orderBy(AUTHOR.LAST_NAME.asc()
```

As you can see, the syntax is quite close to actual SQL. You might be wondering where the AUTHOR object and its properties come from. They come from code generated by jOOQ. The code generation process can be automated with Maven. The following code shows how to configure the `jooq-codegen-maven` plugin in your `pom.xml`:

```
<plugin>
    <groupId>org.jooq</groupId>
    <artifactId>jooq-codegen-maven</artifactId>
    <version>3.9.5</version>
    <executions>
        <execution>
            <goals>
                <goal>generate</goal>
            </goals>
        </execution>
```

```
        </executions>
        <configuration>
            <jdbc>
                <url>${datasource.url}</url>
                <user>${datasource.username}</user>
                <password>${datasource.password}</password>
            </jdbc>
            <generator>
                <database>
                    <name>org.jooq.util.h2.H2Database</name>
                </database>
                <target>
                    <packageName>packt.vaadin.datacentric.chapter06.jooq
                    </packageName>
                    <directory>target/generated-sources/jooq</directory>
                </target>
            </generator>
        </configuration>
    </plugin>
```

You have to configure the connection properties so that the generator can scan the database schema. You also have to configure the database to use it (H2, in this example). Finally, you have to configure the package to be used for the generated code and the directory inside your project where this package is going to reside.

There's one small detail, though. We are using expressions (such as ${datasource.url}) to specify the database connection properties. How can you use values coming from a .properties file inside the pom.xml file? By using the properties-maven-plugin Maven plugin:

```
<plugin>
    <groupId>org.codehaus.mojo</groupId>
    <artifactId>properties-maven-plugin</artifactId>
    <version>1.0.0</version>
    <executions>
        <execution>
            <phase>initialize</phase>
            <goals>
                <goal>read-project-properties</goal>
            </goals>
            <configuration>
                <files>
                <file>src/main/resources/datasource.properties</file>
                </files>
            </configuration>
        </execution>
```

```
        </executions>
    </plugin>
```

With the previous configuration, Maven will be able to read the properties in
the `datasource.properties` file and replace the corresponding expressions in
the `pom.xml` file.

After configuring this two Maven plugins, you can run `mvn clean package` to reverse-
engineer the database schema and generate the corresponding code.

Running queries

You can run queries with jOOQ by creating a `DSLContext` instance. One way of getting this
instance is with the `DSL.using` method:

```
Connection connection = pool.getConnection();
DSLContext dslContext = DSL.using(connection);
```

With this, you can easily run queries using the fluent API offered by jOOQ. For example, to
get all the rows in the messages table, you can use the following:

```
List<MessagesRecord> messages = dslContext.select()
        .from(MESSAGES)
        .fetchInto(MessagesRecord.class);
```

The `MessagesRecord` class and `MESSAGES` instance are provided by the code generated by
jOOQ. This makes the previous query type-safe.

> If, for some reason, your database schema changes, you'll get a
> compilation error and will have the chance to fix the problem before
> deploying it to production. This is one of the strengths of jOOQ.

From here, you can imagine how to implement a `MessageRepository` class using jOOQ.
Here's the solution to such a puzzle, though:

```
public class MessageRepository {

    public static List<MessagesRecord> findAll() {
        try {
            return JooqService.runWithDslContext(context ->
                    context.select()
                            .from(MESSAGES)
                            .fetchInto(MessagesRecord.class)
```

```
            );

        } catch (SQLException e) {
            e.printStackTrace();
            return Collections.emptyList();
        }
    }

    public static void save(MessagesRecord message) {
        try {
            JooqService.runWithDslContext(context ->
                    context.insertInto(MESSAGES, MESSAGES.CONTENT)
                            .values(message.getContent())
                            .execute()
            );

        } catch (SQLException e) {
            e.printStackTrace();
        }
    }

}
```

And the convenient `JooqService.runWithDslContext` method:

```
public class JooqService {
    ...

    public static <T> T runWithDslContext(Function<DSLContext, T>
      function) throws SQLException {
        try (Connection connection = pool.getConnection(); DSLContext
          dslContext = DSL.using(connection)) {
            T t = function.apply(dslContext);
            return t;
        }
    }
}
```

 If you are interested in jOOQ, you might want to evaluate *Ebean* (http://ebean-orm.github.io) and *Querydsl* (http://www.querydsl.com), which are both ORM frameworks that also allow you to implement type-safe queries in Java.

Summary

This chapter was full of new technologies! We discussed what an object-relational mapping framework is, and studied practical examples on how to use three popular persistence technologies for Java: JPA, MyBatis, and jOOQ. We saw how Vaadin Framework allows us to consume any kind of Java API directly, usually through custom abstractions that encapsulate details (such as service and repository classes). We learned the most basic form of data binding in Vaadin, which consists of setting and getting the values directly from domain objects to UI components. We also learned how to separate code that builds up the UI from the code, which adds behavior to it in order to improve its maintainability.

In Chapter 7, *Implementing CRUD User Interfaces*, we are going to see more Vaadin-related topics and discuss data binding in more depth.

Implementing CRUD User Interfaces

7

Most business applications have to deal with data manipulation. Users are able to see, change, delete, and add data. All these actions are executed according to and in the context of a set of rules dictated by the business. In its more fundamental form, business applications include graphical user interfaces to perform CRUD actions over the data. **CRUD** is an acronym for **Create, Read, Update, and Delete**. This chapter explores the design and implementation of CRUD views.

We'll start with a quick discussion about CRUD views from a **User Experience (UX)** perspective. Then, we will move on to how to design and implement CRUD user interfaces using two different UI designs. This chapter also explains the basics of data binding, shows how to use the Java Bean Validation API, and demonstrates how to render UI components inside `Grid` components.

This chapter covers the following topics:

- CRUD user interface design
- Data binding
- Validating with JSR-303
- Grid renderers
- Filtering

Technical requirements

You will be required to have Java SE Development Kit and Java EE SDK version 8 or later. You also need Maven version 3 or later. A Java IDE with Maven support, such as IntelliJ IDEA, Eclipse, or NetBeans is recommended. Finally, to use the Git repository of this book, you need to install Git.

The code files of this chapter can be found on GitHub:
`https://github.com/PacktPublishing/Data-centric-Applications-with-Vaadin-8/`
`tree/master/chapter-07`

Check out the following video to see the code in action:
`https://goo.gl/szGaRy`

CRUD user interface design

UX in the context of **user interfaces** (**UI**) refers to the degree of quality in the interaction between the user and the UI. An application designed with UX in mind enhances the user satisfaction by improving its usability. Simplicity is key in the process of UX design, but avoid falling into a minimalistic design, which may otherwise spoil usability.

 You can find more information about simplicity, minimalism, and general myths about UX design at `http://uxmyths.com`.

UX design may include several disciplines, including wireframing, prototyping, testing, and validating designs. In this section, we'll explore variations of typical CRUD views. Examples of this kind of views are the admin views for managing registered users, views for internal application configuration, or views used by **DevOps** members.

 DevOps is a softwares engineering discipline that unifies software development and software operation (deployment and infrastructure management).

We'll avoid the term CRUD for more sophisticated views that might include all of the CRUD operations. In general, these views are business-specific, and developers should design them according to the particularities of each case.

CRUD views are about *record* editing. Records are items that are usually understood as a whole. Some are suitable for tabular presentation, while others are not; for example, events on a calendar. When designing a CRUD view, think about the following factors:

- **Record complexity**: How many fields does the record contain? Do the fields change depending on the state of other fields? Are there any complex fields such as maps or calendars? How complex are the validation rules?

- **Editing frequency**: How often do users need to edit the record? Do they need a quick way to edit certain fields?
- **Context awareness**: Do users need extra data when editing a record? Do they need, or would they benefit from, seeing other records when editing one?

As a rule of thumb, think about how frequently users will perform the actions on the view, and if they can benefit from seeing many records at a time or not. If the frequency is high for any operation, and they won't benefit from seeing other records in the view, don't use a *generic* CRUD interface. Implement the view tailored to the use case.

Let's analyze three CRUD user interface designs: in-place fields, modal pop-up windows, and hierarchical menus.

In-place fields

With this design, users can activate a field to edit a single value. Data can be presented in a tabular format, in which case, clicking a cell would activate an input field, which would allow the user to directly edit the value. The following figure shows an example of this kind of interface:

Column 1	Column 2	Column 3		Column 4
Value	Value	Value		Value
Value	Value	select	▼	Value
Value	Value	option		Value
		option		
Value	Value	option		Value
Value	Value	option		Value
		option		
		option		

Add

The **Vaadin Framework** allows this through the `Grid.addComponentColumn` method. The following line adds a `Button` to an existing `Grid`:

```
grid.addComponentColumn(user -> new Button("Delete", e ->
deleteClicked(user)));
```

There are advantages and disadvantages of using this option. The main advantage is speed. Users can quickly edit a value, and there's no need to navigate to other views in order to edit the data; however, implementing the `add` operation requires extra considerations. When the user clicks the **Add** button, a new empty row is added; however, it's not easy to know when the row can be saved (in a database, for example). Is a completely empty row a valid record? One way of solving this is by only persisting the record when all the values in it are valid. Another disadvantage is evident when the record has many fields, which, in this case, means a grid with many columns. Editing the data in columns that are scrolled out of the view requires extra interaction from the user, which wipes out the advantage of editing data quickly.

Modal pop-up windows

This kind of user interface shows a modal window anytime the user wants to create, modify, or delete a record. A first approach to this is to combine in-place editors with modal windows. When the user clicks or double-clicks a row, an editor is placed on top of the row, showing all the input fields required to edit the data, and the buttons to cancel the action or save the data. This is exactly what `Grid` editors are in Vaadin Framework, as shown in the following screenshot:

First Name	Last Name	Email	Password	Blocked
First1	Last1	user1@test.com	********	false
First2	Last2	user2@test.com	••••••••	☑
				Save Cancel
First5	Last5	user5@test.com	********	false
First6	Last6	user6@test.com	********	false
First7	Last7	user7@test.com	********	true

This is enabled as follows:

```
grid.getEditor().setEnabled(true);
```

A second approach is to actually show a modal window that blocks any other interaction with other parts of the page. The following is a figure of this kind of interface:

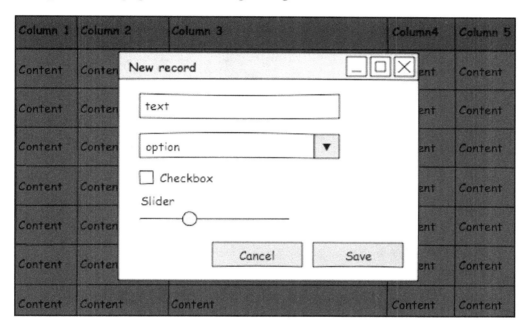

There are several advantages of this approach. The window allows any kind of design for the form it contains. Input fields can be grouped if they are related, help text or instructions can be added, and validation errors can be shown in multiple ways. It is also an intuitive *dead-end view*; users cannot navigate anywhere else but back, which makes it an easy-to-use interaction.

Hierarchical menus

When data can be represented in a hierarchical way, it can serve as the *Read* part in CRUD, and as a navigation tool. The following figure shows a CRUD of *Organizations, Departments,* and *Employees* records:

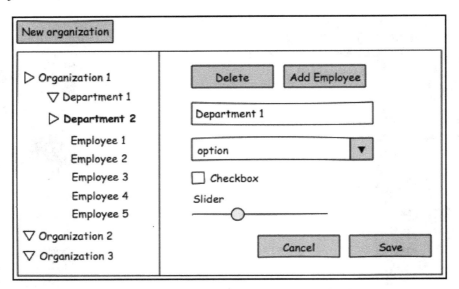

A key element in this kind of design is the use of most of the available space for the forms containing the input fields. Forms are shown in *view mode,* and are made editable when the user clicks an **edit** button. In the preceding figure, a short representation of the records appears in the navigation menu itself. In order to edit one record, the user can click it from the menu. When a record can be associated with one or many records of another type, they are grouped and shown in a hierarchical fashion in the menu. Top-level items in the menu don't necessarily need to be records themselves, since they can serve as a different kind of grouping. For example, a top item could show the **Organizations** option having all the actual organization records as *children.*

This kind of design works well for configuration options; however, it has the disadvantage of showing many options at the same time, which might cause a distraction for end users. For example, a user might forget to click the **Save** button after editing some fields.

The domain model

The following sections show how to implement CRUD views using two different designs: a `Grid` in editable mode, and modal windows. But first, we need to implement a **domain model**. We'll use JPA and *repository classes*, which we explained in the previous chapters. The domain model consists of simple classes to model a role-based schema: `User`, and `Role`. It also includes the corresponding `UserRepository` and `RoleRepository` classes.

Let's start with the simplest of the classes, `Role`. The following is the full implementation of this class:

```
@Entity
@Data
public class Role {

    @Id
    @GeneratedValue
    private Long id;

    private String name;

    private Boolean module1Authorized;

    private Boolean module2Authorized;

    @Override
    public String toString() {
        return name;
    }
}
```

Besides the usual JPA configuration stuff (such as the `@Entity`, `@Id`, and `@GeneratedValue` annotations), the most interesting thing in this class is that there are no `getters` and `setters`. Nevertheless, `getters` and `setters` for each Java field in the class exist! This is thanks to *Project Lombok*, a library that reduces the amount of boilerplate code needed in Java programs. Lombok generates code at the class level. In the previous class, we used the `@Data` annotation in order to tell Lombok to generate `getters` and `setters`, and `toString`, `equals`, and `hashCode` methods. Since the `toString` method generated by Lombok doesn't fit our requirements, we override it and provided a custom one.

In order to use Lombok, you need to install it in your IDE, and add the dependency to the `pom.xml` file:

```
<dependency>
    <groupId>org.projectlombok</groupId>
    <artifactId>lombok</artifactId>
    <version>1.16.18</version>
    <scope>provided</scope>
</dependency>
```

You can find installation instructions for IntelliJ IDEA, NetBeans, Eclipse, and other IDEs at: `https://projectlombok.org`. After installing Lombok, you'll be able to use `autocomplete` and any other features of your IDE in order to use the generated code, even when you don't see it in the Java class. For example, the following screenshot shows **IntelliJ IDEA** suggesting the generated `getName` method when using the autocomplete feature:

```
@Override
public String toString() {
    return getN;
}
    m  getName()                                                          String
    GetNameSpaceMessage (sun.plugin2.message)
    GetMethodFromPropertyName (org.hibernate.validator.internal.ut...
    Press ^Space to see non-imported classes >>                              π
```

You can use your own implementations for the `getters`, `setters`, `equals`, and `hashCode` instead of using Lombok. Most IDEs, if not all of them have features to generate these methods at the source code level; however, Lombok source files become much shorter, making them easier to maintain in most cases. `@Data` is not the only useful annotation offered by Lombok. See the documentation at `https://projectlombok.org` for more information about its features.

The following is the implementation of the `User` class, which uses Lombok as well:

```
@Entity
@Data
public class User {

    @Id
    @GeneratedValue
    private Long id;

    private String firstName;
```

```
        private String lastName;

        private String email;

        private String password;

        private boolean blocked;

        @ManyToMany(fetch = FetchType.EAGER)
        private Set<Role> roles;

        @ManyToOne
        private Role mainRole;
}
```

Notice the @ManyToMany annotation in the roles field. What's the difference between @ManyToMany and @OneToMany? The -ToMany part means that every User can be associated with many Role objects. The @Many- part means that every Role can have many User instances. If @OneToMany was used, the @One- part would mean that every Role can be associated with only one User, which is clearly not what we want in this model.

> Why does the @ManyToMany annotation specify FetchType.EAGER for the fetch strategy? Hibernate uses Fetch.LAZY by default, which might cause a LazyInitializationException. Lazy fetch can be useful if you want to load the data when it is actually needed. This, however, requires an open Hibernate session when the collection is accessed. In a web environment, the session is usually closed after the request is handled. Since we need to show Role data in the views, the best approach is to eagerly fetch the data. A common practice in many applications is to use the *Open Session in View* pattern; however, this might as well be considered an anti-pattern. Always consider using DTO projections instead of the Open Session in the View pattern. For a more detailed discussion about this topic, visit https://vladmihalcea.com/2016/05/30/the-open-session-in-view-anti-pattern.

The last part of the domain model is the repository classes. For the `RoleRepository` class, we only need a method to find all the `Role` objects, and another to save a new one, as shown in the following snippet of code:

```
public class RoleRepository {

    public static List<Role> findAll() { ... }

    public static Role save(Role role) { ... }
}
```

And for completeness, the following are the methods in the `UserRepository` class:

```
public class UserRepository {

    public static List<User> findAll() { ... }

    public static User findById(Long id) { ... }

    private static User getById(Long id, EntityManager em) { ... }

    public static User save(User user) { ... }

    public static void delete(User user) { ... }
}
```

The actual implementation of the methods is omitted here for simplicity, but you can find the complete source code of this chapter's example in the `Data-centric-Applications-with-Vaadin-8\chapter-07` Maven project of the source code that accompanies this book.

Implementing a CRUD using an editable Grid component

In this section, we'll implement a component containing an editable `Grid`. The following is a screenshot of the application showing the `Grid` component in edit mode:

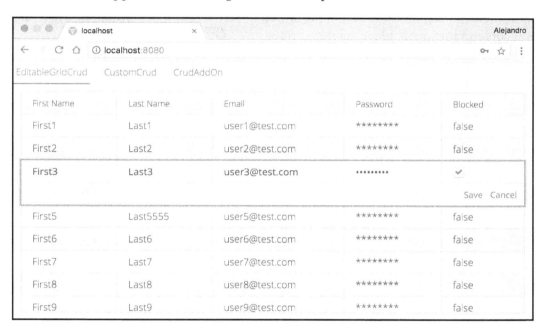

For simplicity, in this example, we'll omit the *add* and the *delete* CRUD operations for now. Let's start by creating a class to encapsulate the component as follows:

```
public class EditableGridCrud extends Composite {

    private Grid<User> grid = new Grid<>();

    public EditableGridCrud() {
        initLayout();
        initBehavior();
    }

    private void initLayout() {
        grid.setSizeFull();
        VerticalLayout layout = new VerticalLayout(grid);
```

```
            setCompositionRoot(layout);
            setSizeFull();
    }

    private void initBehavior() {
    }
}
```

The class, which extends `Composite`, declares a `Grid` to show `User` instances. There are several constructors available in the `Grid` class:

- `Grid()`: Creates a new `Grid`, without columns. Columns have to be manually added.
- `Grid(String caption)`: The same as `Grid()`, but sets a caption.
- `Grid(Class<T> beanType)`: Creates a new `Grid` and automatically creates columns for each property (having a `getter` and a `setter`) in the specified class. Columns can be retrieved by a name using the `getColumn(String)` method.
- `Grid(DataProvider<T, ?> dataProvider)`: Creates a new `Grid` without columns. It accepts a `DataProvider`, which is an abstraction to provide data from any kind of backend. You can implement this interface, or use the implementations available in the framework. If you are not familiar with data providers, refer to the official documentation at: `https://vaadin.com/docs/v8/framework/datamodel/datamodel-providers.html`.
- `Grid(String caption, DataProvider<T, ?> dataProvider)`: The same as `Grid(DataProvider)`, but sets a caption.
- `Grid(String caption, Collection<T> items)`: Creates a new `Grid` without columns, and sets a caption. The provided collection is used to fetch the data that is going to be rendered in the `Grid` (a `DataProvider` is used behind the scenes).

At this point, we have a `Grid` component without columns and without rows (data).

Implementing the read operation

The *read* CRUD operation can be thought of as the action of showing all the `User` instances inside the `Grid`.

Since the `Grid` doesn't have any columns at this point, adding rows to it won't make any difference, so let's start by adding columns. The easiest way to add columns to a `Grid` is by passing the type of the bean (`User`) to the `Grid` constructor:

```
Grid grid = new Grid(User.class);
```

After this, we can add columns by using the property names in the bean. For example:

```
grid.setColumns("firstName", "lastName");
```

However, this is not type-safe. When manually adding columns to a `Grid`, a better approach is not to use the `Grid(Class<T> beanType)` constructor, and instead use a `ValueProvider`. Let's do this in the example application:

```
public class EditableGridCrud extends Composite {
    ...

    private void initBehavior() {
        grid.addColumn(User::getFirstName).setCaption("First name");
        grid.addColumn(User::getLastName).setCaption("Last name");
        grid.addColumn(User::getEmail).setCaption("Email");
        grid.addColumn(User::getPassword).setCaption("Password");
        grid.addColumn(User::isBlocked).setCaption("Blocked");
    }
}
```

This is a better approach, since it's completely type-safe. The `addColumn` method accepts a `ValueProvider`, a functional interface compatible with any getter in the bean type. The `addColumn` method returns an instance of `Grid.Column`, from which we can configure any additional properties for it. In the previous snippet of code, we configured the column's caption. All the `setXX` methods return the same instance of `Column`, which allows you to chain calls to further configure the column. For example, you can set the column's caption and width as follows:

```
grid.addColumn(User::getFirstName)
    .setCaption("First name")
    .setWidth(150);
```

With the columns in place, we can now add rows to the `Grid`. This is as simple as calling the `setItems(Collection)` method, and passing a `Collection` of `User` instances. Since we will need to reload the content of the `Grid` after editing a row, it's a good idea to encapsulate the call to `setItems` as follows:

```
public class EditableGridCrud extends Composite {
    ...

    public EditableGridCrud() {
        initLayout();
        initBehavior();
        refresh();
    }

    private void refresh() {
        grid.setItems(UserRepository.findAll());
    }
    ...

}
```

There's a slight security problem at this point, and by "slight", I mean "major". Passwords are shown in plain text in the `Grid`. We want to keep the **Password** column, so that it plays nice with the `Grid` editor later, but we want to show a series of asterisks (`********`) instead of the actual passwords. This can be done through the `Renderer` interface. A `Renderer` is an extension that *draws* client-side representations of a value. We can use the provided `TextRenderer` implementation to change the text shown in the **Password** column as follows:

```
grid.addColumn(User::getPassword)
        .setCaption("Password")
        .setRenderer(user -> "********", new TextRenderer());
```

The `setRenderer` method accepts a `ValueProvider` and a `Renderer`. Instead of returning `user.getPassword()`, we return the `"********"` string, no matter what the value of the password is. `TextRenderer` will take the string, and *draw* it as text. There are many other `Renderer`s that would take the value and draw it in many other forms; for example, as a `Button` or `HTML`. The following figure shows the implementations included with the framework:

Implementing the update operation

The update CRUD operation is implemented through the `Grid.Editor` class. Enabling the editor is as easy as calling the following:

```
grid.getEditor().setEnabled(true);
```

However, the `Editor` needs a way to know what kind of input component to use for each column, and also where to get the values for these input components, and how to set the values back in the bean once the user edits them. This is done with the help of two methods: `Grid.Editor.getBinder`, and `Grid.Column.setEditorBinding`. You should be familiar with the `Binder` class in the Vaadin Framework; it is a utility class that allows you to connect `setters` and `getters` with input components, as well as validators, converters, and other configurations for *data-binding*. You can get the `Binder` instance by calling the `getBinder` method:

```
Binder<User> binder = grid.getEditor().getBinder();
```

The basic idea of the `Binder` class is that you can specify an input component and bind a getter and a setter:
`binder.bind(textField, User::getFirstName,`
`User::setLastName);`.
If you are not familiar with the `Binder` class, go through the must-read documentation at: `https://vaadin.com/docs/v8/framework/datamodel/` `datamodel-forms.html`.

With the `Editor` enabled, we can set an input component for each column. For example, we can use a `TextField` for the **First Name** column using the `setEditorBinding` method as follows:

```
grid.addColumn(User::getFirstName)
    .setCaption("First Name")
    .setEditorBinding(binder
        .forField(new TextField())
        .bind(User::getFirstName, User::setFirstName));
```

The `setEditorBinding` accepts a `Binding` instance that we can easily get from the `binder`. We use the `forField` method in the `Binder` to specify a new `TextField`, and the `bind` method, which returns an instance of `Binding`, to configure the corresponding `getter` and setter in the `User` bean. The end result is that when you double-click a row in the `Grid`, the `Editor` will present a new `TextField` in the first name cell, which will set its value to what `User::getFirstName` returns, and will call `User::setFirstName`, passing the value in the `TextField` when you click the **Save** button.

Be careful when you set several editor bindings and copy/paste code. You might forget to change one of the three method references, which would result in strange behaviors, such as values not being updated or values being updated in wrong fields in the bean.

In order to persist the edited `User` instance, we need to add an `EditorSaveListener`, which, conveniently, is a functional interface. We add this listener using the `addSaveListener` as follows:

```
grid.getEditor().addSaveListener(e -> save(e.getBean()));
```

The `save` method can be simply implemented as follows:

```
public class EditableGridCrud extends Composite {
    ...

    private void save(User user) {
        UserRepository.save(user);
        refresh();
    }
    ...
}
```

Adding Bean Validation with JSR-303

JSR-303 is the specification for **Java Bean Validation**. It makes it possible to use annotations such as `@NotNull`, `@Email`, and `@Size` to indicate constraints in a Java Bean. Java Bean Validation is a specification and there are several implementations for it, two of the most popular ones being **Hibernate Validation** and *Apache Bean Validation*. Since we are already using Hibernate in this chapter's example, it makes sense to use Hibernate Validation as well. This is done by adding the `hibernate-validator` dependency in the `pom.xml` file:

```
<dependency>
    <groupId>org.hibernate</groupId>
    <artifactId>hibernate-validator</artifactId>
    <version>6.0.2.Final</version>
</dependency>
```

After this, we can use the annotations available in the `javax.validation.constraints` package in the `User` class. The following code adds *not-null* constraints to the `firstName`, `lastName`, and `password` fields, an *email-format* constraint to the `email` field, and a *size* (or length) constraint to the `password` field:

```
...
public class User {
    ...

    @NotNull
    private String firstName;

    @NotNull
    private String lastName;

    @Email
    private String email;
```

```
@NotNull
@Size(min = 8, max = 100)
private String password;

    . . .

}
```

In order to make it work with the `Editor`, we need to add `BeanValidators` to its `Binder`. The following snippet of code shows how to add it to the **First Name** column:

```
grid.addColumn(User::getFirstName)
        .setCaption("First Name")
        .setEditorBinding(binder
                .forField(new TextField())
                .withNullRepresentation("")
                .withValidator(new BeanValidator(User.class, "firstName"))
                .bind(User::getFirstName, User::setFirstName));
```

Notice that we also called `withNullRepresentation`. This allows us to use an empty `String` on the client side, and interpret them as null values on the server side. The `BeanValidator` implementation is provided by the framework, and will take care of running validations for each JavaBean Validation annotation in the `User` class.

Unfortunately, you have to specify the name of the property as a `String` literal, which is not type-safe, and might lead to problems if you forget to update it when you refactor the name of the property. On the other hand, modern IDEs are capable of suggesting such changes when you use the tools for refactoring Java identifiers.

You can use the same approach to configure the `Editor` for the rest of the columns in the `Grid`.

As an exercise, try implementing the `add` operation by creating a button to add a new empty row. When the button is clicked, you can create and persist a new `User` (you will have to set default values for the `firstName`, `lastName`, and `password` fields of the `User` class), refresh the `Grid`, and open the editor for the new `User` using the `grid.getEditor().editRow(rowIndex)` method.

Implementing a CRUD using Grids and forms

In this section, we'll develop a CRUD user interface using modal pop-up windows to show a form for adding and editing `User` instances. The following is a screenshot of the finished form:

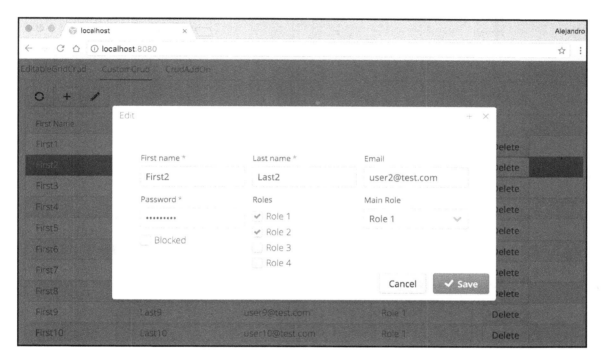

Let's start with the following component:

```
public class CustomCrud extends Composite {

    private Button refresh = new Button("", VaadinIcons.REFRESH);
    private Button add = new Button("", VaadinIcons.PLUS);
    private Button edit = new Button("", VaadinIcons.PENCIL);

    private Grid<User> grid = new Grid<>(User.class);

    public CustomCrud() {
        initLayout();
        initBehavior();
```

```
            refresh();
    }

    private void initLayout() {
        CssLayout header = new CssLayout(refresh, add, edit);
        header.addStyleName(ValoTheme.LAYOUT_COMPONENT_GROUP);

        grid.setSizeFull();

        VerticalLayout layout = new VerticalLayout(header, grid);
        layout.setExpandRatio(grid, 1);
        setCompositionRoot(layout);
        setSizeFull();
    }

    private void initBehavior() {
    }

    public void refresh() {
    }
}
```

There are a few things to take notice of here. We are using the `Grid(Class<T> beanType)` constructor, which means columns are created automatically, and we'll be able to reference them later by name. We are using the `VaadinIcons` class to set icons instead of text for the refresh (read), add, and update buttons. This class is included in the Vaadin Framework. Finally, we are using a `CssLayout` with the `LAYOUT_COMPONENT_GROUP` style, which makes the buttons look like a toolbar. The following is a screenshot of the component at this point:

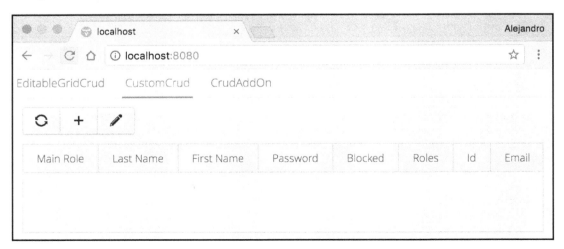

Implementing the read operation

We can start by configuring the columns we actually want to show in the `Grid`. Since the columns were automatically created by the constructor, we can set their visibility by name using the `setColumns` method:

```
    . . .
    private void initLayout() {
        . . .
        grid.setColumns("firstName", "lastName", "email", "mainRole");
        . . .
    }
    . . .
```

In contrast to the previous editable `Grid`, we don't need the *Password* column here, since we are not using an `Editor`.

We can continue by adding a click listener to the `refresh` button, and implementing the `refresh` method. This is pretty straightforward:

```
    . . .
    private void initBehavior() {
        grid.asSingleSelect().addValueChangeListener(e -> updateHeader());
        refresh.addClickListener(e -> refresh());
    }

    public void refresh() {
        grid.setItems(UserRepository.findAll());
        updateHeader();
    }

    private void updateHeader() {
        boolean selected = !grid.asSingleSelect().isEmpty();
        edit.setEnabled(selected);
    }
    . . .
```

We introduced a new `updateHeader` method to enable or disable the `edit` button depending on the selection state in the `Grid`. It makes sense to have the `edit` button enabled only when there's a row selected. We need to call this method when we refresh the list and when the value selected in the `Grid` changes (see the `Grid.addValueChangeListener` method).

Implementing the create and update operations

The *create* CRUD operation starts when the user clicks the add button. Similarly, the *update* CRUD operation starts when the user clicks the update button. We need the following *infrastructure* code:

```
...
private void initBehavior() {
    ...
    add.addClickListener(e -> showAddWindow());
    edit.addClickListener(e -> showEditWindow());
}

private void showAddWindow() {
    UserFormWindow window = new UserFormWindow("Add", new User());
    getUI().addWindow(window);
}

private void showEditWindow() {
    UserFormWindow window = new UserFormWindow("Edit",
grid.asSingleSelect().getValue());
    getUI().addWindow(window);
}
```

When any of the buttons is clicked, we show a UserFormindow (implemented shortly). For the add button, we pass a new User instance. For the update button, we pass the User instance selected in the Grid. We can implement UserWindow as an inner class inside CustomCrud. We'll omit the details of the layout configuration, and focus on the data binding part. Let's start with the following:

```
private class UserFormWindow extends Window { // inner to CustomCrud

    private TextField firstName = new TextField("First name");
    private TextField lastName = new TextField("Last name");
    private TextField email = new TextField("Email");
    private PasswordField password = new PasswordField("Password");
    private CheckBoxGroup<Role> roles = new CheckBoxGroup<>("Roles",
RoleRepository.findAll());
    private ComboBox<Role> mainRole = new ComboBox<>("Main Role",
RoleRepository.findAll());
    private CheckBox blocked = new CheckBox("Blocked");

    private Button cancel = new Button("Cancel");
    private Button save = new Button("Save", VaadinIcons.CHECK);

    public UserFormWindow(String caption, User user) {
```

```
        initLayout(caption);
        initBehavior(user);
    }

    private void initLayout(String caption) {
        ...
    }

    private void initBehavior(User user) {
    }
}
```

All the input fields in the form are members of the UserFormWindow class, and are added to some sort of layout in the initLayout method (not shown).

The initBehaviour method should configure the data binding between the User instance and the input fields. It also should add behavior to the cancel and save buttons. Let's think about what's required before we start coding:

- We need data-binding. In the Vaadin Framework, that usually means using a Binder.

- We need to bind the fields in the UserFormWindow class to the fields in the User class.

- We need to make sure that the input fields show the correct values initially.

- We need to make sure that the values in the input fields are written in the User instance when the **save** button is clicked.

- We need to make sure no values are written in the User instance when the **cancel** button is clicked.

Now, we can start coding:

```
private void initBehavior(User user) { // inside UserFormWindow
    Binder<User> binder = new Binder<>(User.class);
    binder.bindInstanceFields(this);
    binder.readBean(user);
}
```

Two important things happen in the previous code: one) all the Java fields that are also input fields in the UserFormWindow class are bound to the Java fields in the User class (with the bindIntanceFields call); and two), all the values in the Java fields of the User class are set to the corresponding input fields in the UserFormWindow class (with the readBean call).

Finally, the following code adds the behavior to the buttons:

```
private void initBehavior(User user) { // inside UserFormWindow
    ...

    cancel.addClickListener(e -> close());
    save.addClickListener(e -> {
        try {
            binder.writeBean(user);
            UserRepository.save(user);
            close();
            refresh();
            Notification.show("User saved");

        } catch (ValidationException ex) {
            Notification.show("Please fix the errors and try again");
        }
    });
}
```

The listener on the `cancel` button only has to call `Window.close()` (inherited). The listener on the `save` button calls `writeBean` in order to write the values in the input fields in the `user` instance.

Notice that `writeBean` throws a `ValidationException`. There are no validations at the moment, though. Adding the JavaBean Validation constraints we have in the `User` class is as simple as changing the `Binder` implementation:

```
private void initBehavior(User user) { // inside UserFormWindow
    BeanValidationBinder<User> binder = new
BeanValidationBinder<>(User.class);
    ...
}
```

Implementing the delete operation

Let's implement the *delete* CRUD operation using a different approach. Instead of simply adding one single button for the operation, we'll add a delete button on each row in the `Grid`. The simplest way of adding a UI component inside a `Grid` is by using the `addComponentColumn` method:

```
public class CustomCrud extends Composite {
    ...
```

```
        private void initLayout() {
            ...

            grid.addComponentColumn(user -> new Button("Delete", e ->
deleteClicked(user)));
            ...
        }
        ...

        private void deleteClicked(User user) {
            showRemoveWindow(user);
            refresh();
        }

        private void showRemoveWindow(User user) {
            Window window = new RemoveWindow(user);
            window.setModal(true);
            window.center();
            getUI().addWindow(window);
        }
    }
}
```

The addComponentColumn method accepts a ValueProvider used to get a UI component. The constructor used to create the Button accepts a click listener that, in turn, calls the showRemoveWindow method, passing the User instance corresponding to the row where the button resides. The actual implementation of the RemoveWindow class is left as an exercise.

 The addComponentColumn method is a shortcut to addColumn(user -> new Button("Delete", e -> deleteClicked(user)), new ComponentRenderer()).

Using the Crud UI add-on

Thanks to its open source nature, there are hundreds of third-party components and utilities published available at: https://vaadin.com/directory. One of them does almost all the work we have done in this chapter. The following class shows how to implement a CRUD user interface using the Crud UI add-on available at https://vaadin.com/directory/component/crud-ui-add-on, which is maintained by the author of this book:

```
    public class CrudAddOn extends Composite {

        private GridCrud<User> crud = new GridCrud<>(User.class, new
```

```
HorizontalSplitCrudLayout());

    public CrudAddOn() {
        initLayout();
        initBehavior();
    }

    private void initLayout() {
        crud.getGrid().setColumns("firstName", "lastName", "email",
"mainRole");
        crud.getCrudFormFactory().setVisibleProperties("firstName",
"lastName", "email", "password", "roles", "mainRole", "blocked");

        crud.getCrudFormFactory().setFieldType("password",
PasswordField.class);
        crud.getCrudFormFactory().setFieldProvider("roles", new
CheckBoxGroupProvider<>(RoleRepository.findAll()));
        crud.getCrudFormFactory().setFieldProvider("mainRole", new
ComboBoxProvider<>("Main Role", RoleRepository.findAll()));

        VerticalLayout layout = new VerticalLayout(crud);
        setCompositionRoot(layout);
        setSizeFull();
    }

    private void initBehavior() {
        crud.setFindAllOperation(() -> UserRepository.findAll());
        crud.setAddOperation(user -> UserRepository.save(user));
        crud.setUpdateOperation(user -> UserRepository.save(user));
        crud.setDeleteOperation(user -> UserRepository.delete(user));
        crud.getCrudFormFactory().setUseBeanValidation(true);
    }
}
```

The add-on offers several configuration options, such as the possibility to configure a layout, set field providers, and use JavaBean Validation. It also delegates the CRUD operations to your own code, allowing you to use any kind of Java backend technology. The following is a screenshot of the CRUD component created with the Crud UI add-on:

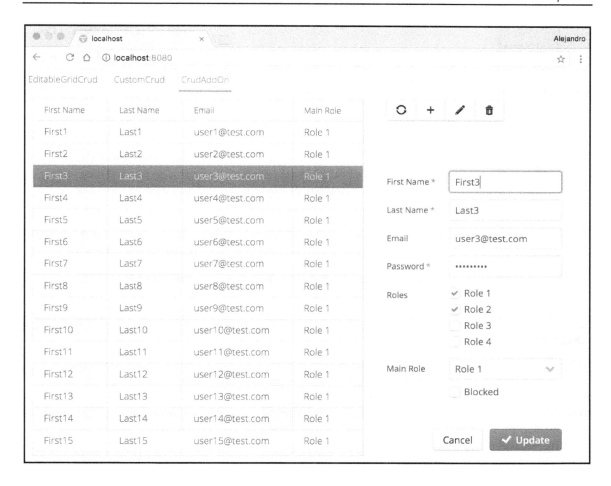

Filtering

Filtering can be implemented by adding UI components such as a `TextField` and
a `ComoboBox` with value listeners on them. When the user changes the filtering
components, the value listeners update the data by passing their values to the backend and
updating the view accordingly. For example, in order to filter by last name,
the `UserRepository.findAll` method should accept a string with the value to match:

```
public class UserRepository {

    public static List<User> findAll(String lastName) {
        return JPAService.runInTransaction(em ->
```

```
                    em.createQuery("select u from User u where u.lastName like
 :lastName")
                        .setParameter("lastName", lastName)
                        .getResultList()
            );
    }
    ...
}
```

 Always keep in mind that findAll methods are useful and safe to use when they return a small number of results. When this is not the case, you should add *lazy loading* capabilities like the ones discussed in Chapter 9, *Lazy Loading*.

Assuming there is a lastNameFilter input component (of type TextField, for example), the Grid should be populated using the new method, and passing the value in the filter:

```
grid.setItems(UserRepository.findAll(lastNameFilter.getValue()));
```

Summary

In this chapter, we learned how to implement *generic* CRUD user interfaces. We studied three different UI designs for CRUD user interfaces: in-place fields, modal pop-up windows, and hierarchical menus. We learned about Project Lombok, which allows us to reduce the amount of boilerplate code needed in Java programs, and we implemented a domain model using JPA and JavaBean Validation constraints. We also covered data binding with the Binder class, Grid renderers, and filtering.

In the next chapter, we'll explore another interesting topic that is useful in many business applications: generating and visualizing reports.

Adding Reporting Capabilities

8

Many business applications require the generation of reports as part of their functionality. A *report* is the representation of data in a certain format for a particular audience. A *Report Generator* (or *Report Viewer*) is an application or an application module that allows end users to visualize and download reports. Very often, a report generator takes data from a database and produces a document in a format suitable for printing on paper. We will focus on this type of report generator in this chapter. There are many ready-to-use report generators with advanced features, such as business intelligence and analytics, but these systems are out of the scope of this book.

In this chapter, we'll learn how to render `JasperReports` in a Vaadin application without having to deal with report designers or XML design formats. Instead, we'll use a Java API to design the reports, similarly to how you use Java to design a web UI using Vaadin Framework. We'll also discuss background report generation and Server Push, a mechanism that allows us to update the client from a separate thread running on the server.

This chapter covers the following topics:

- Integrating `JasperReports` with Vaadin
- Rendering runtime-generated HTML
- Long-running background tasks
- Server Push

Technical requirements

You will be required to have Java SE Development Kit and Java EE SDK version 8 or later. You also need Maven version 3 or later. A Java IDE with Maven support, such as IntelliJ IDEA, Eclipse, or NetBeans is recommended. Finally, to use the Git repository of this book, you need to install Git.

The code files of this chapter can be found on GitHub:
`https://github.com/PacktPublishing/Data-centric-Applications-with-Vaadin-8/tree/master/chapter-08`

Check out the following video to see the code in action:
`https://goo.gl/9sdD5q`

The example application

Throughout the chapter, we'll develop a **Report Viewer**. The following is a screenshot of the finished application:

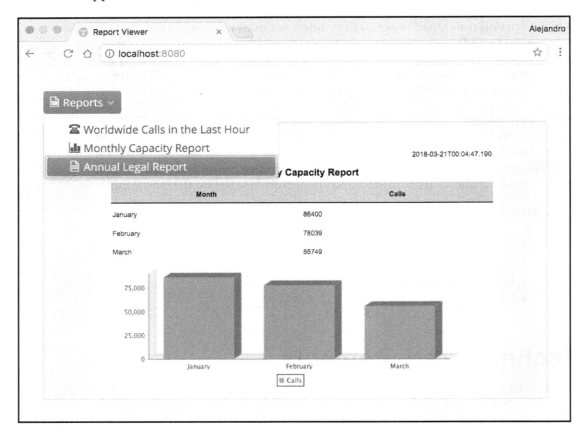

The data model

The data model is based on a simple SQL table, `Call`, that contains columns for the ID, client name, phone number, city, start time, duration, and status. The following is a JPA Entity representing this table:

```
@Entity
@Data
public class Call {

    @Id
    @GeneratedValue
    private Long id;

    private String client;

    private String phoneNumber;

    @Enumerated(EnumType.STRING)
    private City city;

    private LocalDateTime startTime;

    private Integer duration;

    @Enumerated(EnumType.STRING)
    private Status status;
}
```

`Status` and `City` are simple Java `enums` that define some test values:

```
public enum Status {
    RECEIVED, MISSED
}

public enum City {
    BOGOTA, TURKU, LONDON, BERLIN, HELSINKI, TOKYO, SAN_FRANCISCO, SIDNEY,
    LAGOS, VANCOUVER, SANTIAGO, BEIJING
}
```

Notice the `@Enumerated` annotations in the `city` and `status` fields of the `Call` class. This is used to persist the value as a string in the database instead of an integer representing the value, which allows us to use simpler SQL queries for the reports.

We'll use two persistence frameworks in this application. For parts of the application that require saving data or running business logic, we'll use JPA. For reports data, we'll use MyBatis. In your applications you can, of course, use only one framework. The reason behind choosing MyBatis for report generation is that it's a great fit for constructing and maintaining complex SQL queries. SQL, in turn, is a powerful language and a perfect fit for reporting. The ability to copy an SQL query from your code and run it directly on a SQL client eases implementation and maintenance as you can quickly see the data you'd get in a report without having to compile or execute the application. Each report has its own **data transfer model** (**DTO**), a class that encapsulates the data to be rendered in a report in a convenient format. The advantage of this is that we don't have to query extra data not used in the report and so free the web server from data processing to some extent.

The configuration of both frameworks is implemented in the JPAService and MyBatisService classes and the persistence.xml and mybatis-config.xml files. A file-based H2 database is used by default, but you'll find configuration examples for MySQL and PostgreSQL as comments in the configuration files.

You can find the complete source code of this chapter's example in the Data-centric-Applications-with-Vaadin-8\chapter-08 Maven project of the source code that accompanies this book.

Since a report viewer doesn't make sense without data, the example application includes a random data generator that populates the Call table with random data. When the table is empty, the generator will fill it with initial data representing phone calls made in the past 6 months at a rate of one million calls per year. If the table is not empty, the generator will "fill" the time span between the time of the last call in the table and the current time using the same rate. Additionally, the generator runs a background thread that inserts random data at runtime. This generator is meant to simulate a real-life situation in which data is constantly inserted into the database, sometimes even when the application is not running. You can find the implementation in the DataGenerator class.
The DataGenerator functionality is invoked from a ServletContextListener that is defined in the WebConfig class. The initial time span and the rate used in the generator is configurable via parameters, in case you want to use different values.

The Vaadin UI

The VaadinServlet is configured in the WebConfig class. The UI implementation is realized in the VaadinUI class. For reference, the following snippet of code shows the implementation of the layout of the example application:

```
@Title("Report Viewer")
public class VaadinUI extends UI {

    private HorizontalLayout header = new HorizontalLayout();
    private Panel panel = new Panel();
    private MenuBar.MenuItem annualLegalReportItem;

    @Override
    protected void init(VaadinRequest vaadinRequest) {
        MenuBar menuBar = new MenuBar();
        menuBar.addStyleName(ValoTheme.MENUBAR_BORDERLESS);
        MenuBar.MenuItem reportsMenuItem = menuBar.addItem("Reports",
VaadinIcons.FILE_TABLE, null);
        reportsMenuItem.addItem("Worldwide Calls in the Last Hour",
VaadinIcons.PHONE_LANDLINE,
                i -> showLastHourCallReport());
        reportsMenuItem.addItem("Monthly Capacity Report",
VaadinIcons.BAR_CHART_H,
                i -> showMonthlyCapacityReport());
        annualLegalReportItem = reportsMenuItem.addItem("Annual Legal
Report", VaadinIcons.FILE_TEXT_O,
                i -> generateAnnualLegalReport());

        header.addComponents(menuBar);

        panel.addStyleName(ValoTheme.PANEL_WELL);

        VerticalLayout mainLayout = new VerticalLayout(header);
        mainLayout.addComponentsAndExpand(panel);
        setContent(mainLayout);
    }
    ...
}
```

We are going to develop three different reports.
The `showLastHourCallReport`, `showMonthlyCapacityReport`,
and `generateAnnualLegalReport` methods include the logic to modify the UI in order to show the respective report inside the `panel` component.

Integrating JasperReports with Vaadin

`JasperReports` is an open-source reporting engine to produce reports that can be rendered in a variety of formats, such as HTML, PDF, Microsoft Excel, ODT (OpenOffice), and others. Typically, reports are designed in a visual editor (iReport Designer) or XML files (JRXML). The design is compiled into a Jasper file (`*.jasper`), filled with data, and exported to the desired format.

`DynamicJasper` and `DynamicReports` are two open-source libraries that abstract away the JRXML format and provide APIs to design reports in Java. This is a good match for the philosophy of the Vaadin Framework which allows you to implement HTML-based web applications in Java. In this chapter, we'll use `DynamicJasper`, but the concepts are similar if you prefer `DynamicReports`. Some of the concepts can be also used if you plan to design reports in JRXML files directly or through the iReport Designer tool.

You can include `DynamicJasper` by adding the following dependency to your `pom.xml` file:

```
<dependency>
    <groupId>ar.com.fdvs</groupId>
    <artifactId>DynamicJasper</artifactId>
    <version>5.1.0</version>
</dependency>
```

In order to export to Microsoft Office formats, you need to add Apache POI as a dependency:

```
<dependency>
    <groupId>org.apache.poi</groupId>
    <artifactId>poi-ooxml</artifactId>
    <version>3.10-FINAL</version>
</dependency>
```

Getting the data

A crucial part of report generation is data gathering. Data is arguably the most important input in a report. Having good "infrastructure code" for data gathering will highly improve maintainability in report modules. In this chapter, we'll use an SQL database, since it's probably the most common kind of data store in use. This means reports are filled with data queried using SQL. Reporting doesn't require saving data, only reading. SQL queries in reports tend to have multiple lines and are sometimes generated dynamically. MyBatis seems to be an excellent choice for reporting modules. MyBatis allows query definition in XML files, which, unlike Java Strings, help with long multi-line SQL queries and dynamic query definitions.

To use XML-based mappers with MyBatis, specify the name of the XML file using the `resource` attribute of the `mapper` element in the MyBatis configuration file:

```
<configuration>
    ...
    <mappers>
        <mapper resource="mappers/ReportsMapper.xml"/>
    </mappers>
</configuration>
```

The `ReportsMapper.xml` file is defined as follows:

```
<?xml version="1.0" encoding="UTF-8" ?>
<!DOCTYPE mapper PUBLIC "-//mybatis.org//DTD Mapper 3.0//EN"
"http://mybatis.org/dtd/mybatis-3-mapper.dtd">

<mapper
namespace="packt.vaadin.datacentric.chapter08.reports.ReportsMapper">
    ...
</mapper>
```

This file defines the mapper Java interface to use. All queries defined inside the `mapper` element are mapped to the corresponding methods in the `ReportsMapper` class. For example, we can define a method to get all the calls before a given time as follows:

```
public interface ReportsMapper {

    List<CallDto> findCallsBefore(LocalDateTime time);
}
```

Notice that we are not using the JPA Entity as a result type. Instead, we are using a DTO with, and only with, the required Java fields to store the data from the SQL query:

```
@Data
public class CallDto {
    private String client;
    private String phoneNumber;
    private City city;
    private LocalDateTime startTime;
    private Integer duration;
    private Status status;
}
```

We can map an SQL query to the `findCallsBefore` method as follows:

```
<mapper
namespace="packt.vaadin.datacentric.chapter08.reports.ReportsMapper">

    <select id="findCallsBefore"
resultType="packt.vaadin.datacentric.chapter08.reports.CallDto">
        SELECT
          city,
          client,
          phoneNumber,
          startTime,
          duration,
          status
        FROM Call
        WHERE startTime >= #{time}
        ORDER BY startTime DESC
    </select>

</mapper>
```

The UI doesn't consume the mapper interface directly. Instead, we can define more high-level methods in a service class. For example, the *Worldwide Calls in the Last Hour* report, the data from which the previous query comes, uses the `lastHourCalls` method in the `ReportsService` class:

```
public class ReportsService {

    public static List<CallDto> lastHourCalls() {
        try (SqlSession session =
MyBatisService.getSqlSessionFactory().openSession()) {
            LocalDateTime startOfHour = LocalDateTime.now().minusHours(1);
            ReportsMapper mapper = session.getMapper(ReportsMapper.class);
            return mapper.findCallsBefore(startOfHour);
```

```
            }
        }
    }
```

This allows for reusing queries when the data is the same but different processing (such as formatting, or computation of input parameters) is required.

Designing the report

Let's start with the implementation of a simple report, the *Worldwide Calls in the Last Hour* report, shown in the following screenshot:

City	Client	Phone number	Date	Start time	Minutes	Status
TOKYO	Alex Allison	555 016 350	2018-02-01	19:58:16.812	0	MISSED
VANCOUVER	Edgar Simpson	555 016 436	2018-02-01	19:57:45.702	14	RECEIVED
BOGOTA	Alex Mattsson	555 011 057	2018-02-01	19:57:14.592	6	RECEIVED
BOGOTA	Marian Brown	555 013 351	2018-02-01	19:56:43.483	0	MISSED
BOGOTA	Joshua Ross	555 011 332	2018-02-01	19:56:12.375	0	MISSED
BERLIN	Alice Simons	555 018 428	2018-02-01	19:55:41.264	0	MISSED
BERLIN	Dan Verne	555 012 041	2018-02-01	19:55:10.153	0	MISSED
SIDNEY	Mike Barks	555 013 406	2018-02-01	19:54:39.045	10	RECEIVED
SAN_FRANCISCO	Joshua Smith	555 018 911	2018-02-01	19:54:07.939	0	MISSED
BERLIN	Edgar Barks	555 011 668	2018-02-01	19:53:36.828	0	MISSED
LONDON	John Scott	555 016 682	2018-02-01	19:53:05.719	0	MISSED
HELSINKI	Peter Scott	555 018 312	2018-02-01	19:52:34.611	0	MISSED
BOGOTA	Peter Simons	555 013 609	2018-02-01	19:52:03.5	0	MISSED
BERLIN	Peter Simons	555 015 572	2018-02-01	19:51:32.391	0	MISSED
TOKYO	Alex Clavel	555 019 922	2018-02-01	19:51:01.285	0	MISSED
BEIJING	Rita Verne	555 010 319	2018-02-01	19:50:30.175	0	MISSED

CONFIDENTIAL 2018-02-01T19:58:28.422
Worldwide Calls in the Last Hour

To create a report using `DynamicJasper`, you have to create an object of type `DynamicReport`. This is done by using the `DynamicReportBuilder` class, which provides methods to add the title, header, columns, and other elements that form the report. The `DynamicReportBuilder` class implements the *builder pattern* to allow creating the report step by step and a method to build the `DynamicReport` instance. There are several subclasses of `DynamicReportBuilder`; we'll follow the examples given in the official documentation and use the `FastReportBuilder` class.

We can start by configuring the title and header information, enabling full page width, setting the text to show when there's no data, and enabling a background color for odd rows:

```
DynamicReport report = new FastReportBuilder()
        .setTitle("Worldwide Calls in the Last Hour")
        .addAutoText("CONFIDENTIAL", AutoText.POSITION_HEADER,
AutoText.ALIGMENT_LEFT, 200, new Style())
        .addAutoText(LocalDateTime.now().toString(),
AutoText.POSITION_HEADER, AutoText.ALIGNMENT_RIGHT, 200, new Style())
        .setUseFullPageWidth(true)
        .setWhenNoData("(no calls)", new Style())
        .setPrintBackgroundOnOddRows(true)
        .build();
```

Notice how, after configuring the report, we end the sentence by calling the `build` method, which returns an instance of `DynamicReport`. All configuration calls happen between the instantiation (`new FastReportBuilder()`) and the call to `build()`.

The report data is defined by columns. Columns are configured with the `addColumn` method. The `addColumn` method accepts an instance of type `AbstractColumn` that we can create by using `ColumnBuilder`, also a builder class. The following snippet of code demonstrates how to create the seven columns that make up the report:

```
DynamicReport report = new FastReportBuilder()
        ...
        .addColumn(ColumnBuilder.getNew()
                .setColumnProperty("city", City.class)
                .setTitle("City")
                .build())
        .addColumn(ColumnBuilder.getNew()
                .setColumnProperty("client", String.class)
                .setTitle("Client")
                .build())
        .addColumn(ColumnBuilder.getNew()
                .setColumnProperty("phoneNumber", String.class)
```

```
                .setTitle("Phone number")
                .build())
        .addColumn(ColumnBuilder.getNew()
                .setColumnProperty("startTime", LocalDateTime.class)
                .setTitle("Date")
                .setTextFormatter(DateTimeFormatter.ISO_DATE.toFormat())
                .build())
        .addColumn(ColumnBuilder.getNew()
                .setColumnProperty("startTime", LocalDateTime.class)
 .setTextFormatter(DateTimeFormatter.ISO_LOCAL_TIME.toFormat())
                .setTitle("Start time")
                .build())
        .addColumn(ColumnBuilder.getNew()
                .setColumnProperty("duration", Integer.class)
                .setTitle("Minutes")
                .build())
        .addColumn(ColumnBuilder.getNew()
                .setColumnProperty("status", Status.class)
                .setTitle("Status").build())
        .build();
```

For each column, we have to specify the name of the corresponding Java property in the `CallDto` class and its type. We can also specify the title and *text formatters* when needed.

The `DynamicReport` instance defines the visual structure of the report. With this in place, we can create a `JasperPrint` object, which represents a page-oriented document that can be later exported to multiple formats. We first need to get the data from the service class, and then pass the `DynamicReport` instance and the data to the `generateJasperPrint` method of the `DynamicJasperHelper` class:

```
List<CallDto> calls = ReportsService.lastHourCalls();
JasperPrint print = DynamicJasperHelper.generateJasperPrint(report, new
ClassicLayoutManager(), calls);
```

Rendering a report as HTML

The `JasperPrint` instance can be exported to several formats. Since we are interested in rendering the report in a Vaadin web application, we can export the report to HTML and use a `Label` configured with `ContentMode.HTML` as follows:

```
ByteArrayOutputStream outputStream = new ByteArrayOutputStream()
HtmlExporter exporter = new HtmlExporter();
exporter.setExporterOutput(new SimpleHtmlExporterOutput(outputStream));
```

```
exporter.setExporterInput(new SimpleExporterInput(print));
exporter.exportReport();

outputStream.flush();
Label htmlLabel = new Label("", ContentMode.HTML);
htmlLabel.setValue(outputStream.toString("UTF-8"));
```

The `HtmlExporter` class sends its output to an `OutputStream`, which we can convert to `String` and set as a `Label` value. This `Label` can be added to any Vaadin layout, as shown in this snippet of code, which also takes into account exception handling and resources:

```
public class LastHourCallReport extends Composite {

    public LastHourCallReport() {
        try (ByteArrayOutputStream outputStream = new
ByteArrayOutputStream()) {
            DynamicReport report = new FastReportBuilder()
                    ...
                    .build();
            ...

            Label htmlLabel = new Label("", ContentMode.HTML);
            htmlLabel.setValue(outputStream.toString("UTF-8"));
            setCompositionRoot(htmlLabel);

        } catch (JRException | IOException e) {
            throw new RuntimeException(e);
        }
    }
}
```

Adding charts

Adding charts with `DynamicJasper` is done through the `addChart` method of the `FastReportBuilder` class. The following snippet of code shows the full configuration of the *Monthly Capacity Report*:

```
DynamicReportBuilder reportBuilder = new FastReportBuilder()
        .setUseFullPageWidth(true)
        .setTitle("Monthly Capacity Report")
        .setWhenNoData("(no data)", new Style())
        .addAutoText("CONFIDENTIAL", AutoText.POSITION_HEADER,
AutoText.ALIGMENT_LEFT, 200, new Style())
        .addAutoText(LocalDateTime.now().toString(),
```

```
AutoText.POSITION_HEADER, AutoText.ALIGNMENT_RIGHT, 200, new Style())
        .addColumn(monthColumn = ColumnBuilder.getNew()
                .setColumnProperty("monthName", String.class)
                .setTitle("Month")
                .build())
        .addColumn(callsColumn = ColumnBuilder.getNew()
                .setColumnProperty("calls", Integer.class)
                .setTitle("Calls")
                .build())
    .addChart(new DJBar3DChartBuilder()
            .setCategory((PropertyColumn) monthColumn)
            .addSerie(callsColumn)
            .build());
```

Notice how we need a reference to the columns containing the data we want to use in the chart. The `setCategory` and `addSeries` methods accept these references.

In order to render charts, we must configure an `ImageServlet`, which is provided by the `JasperReports` library. This servlet serves the images that make up the charts. In the example application for this chapter, the servlet is declared in the `WebConfig` class as a static inner class:

```
@WebServlet("/image")
public static class ReportsImageServlet extends ImageServlet {
}
```

You can use any suitable URL. This needs to be configured in the output used by the exporter class (for example, `HTMLExporter`). Additionally, the `JasperPrint` instance has to be set in the HTTP session. The following snippet of code shows the extra configuration needed when rendering charts:

```
...
JasperPrint print = ...
VaadinSession.getCurrent().getSession().setAttribute(ImageServlet.DEFAULT_J
ASPER_PRINT_SESSION_ATTRIBUTE, print);

SimpleHtmlExporterOutput exporterOutput = ...
exporterOutput.setImageHandler(new
WebHtmlResourceHandler("image?image={0}"));

HtmlExporter exporter = new HtmlExporter();
exporter.setExporterOutput(exporterOutput);
...
```

The `WebHtmlResourceHandler` constructor accepts a string with the URL pattern to use by the internal image handler in the exporter. Notice how the pattern starts with `image`. This is the same value used in the `ImageServlet` mapping.

Generating a report in a background task

Report generation may involve expensive computation due to large amounts of data, connections to external systems, and data processing. In many situations, report data is gathered directly from the original source, typically an SQL database. This has two clear drawbacks. The first problem is that as the application runs, more and more data is added into the database, making reports run slower with time. The second problem is that report generation may heavily use the database at certain times, interfering with the usage of other parts of the application.

One step toward improving this situation is to progressively and continuously generate the data required for reporting. For example, consider the following query that calculates the average on a column:

```
SELECT AVG(column_name) FROM table_name
```

Instead of using this query, you can use the following formula to continuously calculate the average (*an*) from the previous average value (a_{n-1}) every time a new value (x_n) is persisted:

$$a_n = \frac{(n-1)a_{n-1} + x_n}{n}$$

This, of course, doesn't take into account *delete* operations, and requires calculating the average any time a new value is persisted in the database, but the key idea of this simple example is to try to *help* the application to pre-generate data for reporting, as data is added, modified, or deleted in order to minimize the amount of computational power required at report generation time.

When pre-processing data, or when there are computations that depend on time or external data sources, report generation may take longer than a normal request to the application. In these cases, you can use background threads to generate the report and notify the user when the report is ready. In the example application, you can see an **Annual legal report** option in the **Reports** menu. Generating this report is expensive in terms of application time, so instead of locking the application's usage until the report is ready, the application shows a notification saying that the report is being generated and starts the process in a background thread, letting users visualize other reports in the meantime:

When the report is ready, the application notifies you again and shows a button that allows you to download the report:

The next sections explain how to implement this behavior.

Exporting a report to a PDF

HTML is the best option to render a report in a browser. However, `JasperReports` and `DynamicJasper` support many other formats. These formats are available as implementations of the `JRExporter` interface. One of them is the `JRPdfExporter` class. The example application includes the `LastHourCallReport` class, which, in contrast to previous report implementations, is not a Vaadin UI component. Since we want to allow users to download this report, we don't really need a UI component for it. Instead, `LastHourCallReport` is a helper class that configures the report, exports it as a PDF, and exposes the content of the file through an `OutputStream` suitable for the `FileDownloader` class, part of Vaadin Framework.

Omitting the details about the report configuration, which we already covered in previous sections, the following is the implementation of the `LastHourCallReport` class:

```
public class AnnualLegalReport {

    public static ByteArrayOutputStream getOutputStream() {
        try (ByteArrayOutputStream outputStream = new
ByteArrayOutputStream()) {
            DynamicReport report = new FastReportBuilder()
                        ... configure report ...
                        .build();

            List<ClientCountDto> clients =
ReportsService.countYearCallsByClient();
            JasperPrint print =
DynamicJasperHelper.generateJasperPrint(report, new ClassicLayoutManager(),
clients);

            JRPdfExporter exporter = new JRPdfExporter();
            exporter.setExporterOutput(new
SimpleOutputStreamExporterOutput(outputStream));
            exporter.setExporterInput(new SimpleExporterInput(print));
            exporter.exportReport();

            outputStream.flush();
            return outputStream;

        } catch (JRException | IOException e) {
            throw new RuntimeException(e);
        }
    }
}
```

We need to call the `getOutputStream` method from a new thread and modify the UI, also from this new thread, to add a button that downloads the PDF file. In order to modify the UI from a separate thread, we need to enable and use Server Push.

Server Push

Let's examine what happens if we modify the UI from a separate thread without using Server Push:

```java
@Title("Report Viewer")
public class VaadinUI extends UI {

    private HorizontalLayout header = new HorizontalLayout();
    private MenuBar.MenuItem annualLegalReportItem;
    ...

    private void generateAnnualLegalReport() {
        Notification.show("Report generation started",
                "You'll be notified once the report is ready.",
                Notification.Type.TRAY_NOTIFICATION);
        annualLegalReportItem.setEnabled(false);

        new Thread(() -> {
            ByteArrayOutputStream outputStream =
                AnnualLegalReport.getOutputStream();
            ByteArrayInputStream inputStream = new
                ByteArrayInputStream(outputStream.toByteArray());
            Button button = new Button("Download Annual Legal Report",
                VaadinIcons.DOWNLOAD_ALT);
            header.addComponent(button);

            FileDownloader downloader = new FileDownloader(new
                StreamResource(() -> {
                    header.removeComponent(button);
                    annualLegalReportItem.setEnabled(true);
                    return inputStream;
                }, "annual-legal-report.pdf"));
            downloader.extend(button);

            Notification.show("Report ready for download",
                Notification.Type.TRAY_NOTIFICATION);
        }).start();
    }
}
```

When the user clicks the corresponding option in the menu, the generateAnnualLegalReport method is called. The method starts a new thread, so we end up with two threads; the one that started when the HTTP request happened (the menu option is clicked) and the one started by the generateAnnualLegalReport method. When the HTTP request finishes, the user is able to continue using the application in the browser. At some point later, the AnnualLegalReport.getOutputStream() method finishes and the application tries to modify the UI. However, this is happening in a separate background thread in the server. All changes to the UI are lost or may fail, since the thread is not associated with the UI instance, and NullPointerExceptions may be thrown by the framework (this is the case with the Notification.show method).

You can get a lock on the session in order to guarantee a UI instance is available and avoid NullPointerExceptions by wrapping any code that modifies the UI from outside a request-handling thread with the UI.access(Runnable) method:

```
new Thread(() -> {
    ByteArrayOutputStream outputStream =
AnnualLegalReport.getOutputStream();
    ByteArrayInputStream inputStream = new
ByteArrayInputStream(outputStream.toByteArray());
    access(() -> {
        Button button = new Button("Download Annual Legal Report",
VaadinIcons.DOWNLOAD_ALT);
        header.addComponent(button);

        FileDownloader downloader = new FileDownloader(new
StreamResource(() -> {
            header.removeComponent(button);
            annualLegalReportItem.setEnabled(true);
            return inputStream;
        }, "annual-legal-report.pdf"));
        downloader.extend(button);

        Notification.show("Report ready for download",
Notification.Type.TRAY_NOTIFICATION);
    });
}).start();
```

There's still one problem; the server needs to send the changes to the browser, something we can achieve by enabling **Server Push**. Server Push is a technique that starts a communication process from the server to the client, in opposition to a typical HTTP request where the communication is initiated by the client (web browser). In order to use Server Push, you need to add the vaadin-push dependency in your pom.xml file:

```
<dependency>
    <groupId>com.vaadin</groupId>
    <artifactId>vaadin-push</artifactId>
</dependency>
```

To enable Server Push, you can annotate the UI implementation class with @Push:

```
@Push
@Title("Report Viewer")
public class VaadinUI extends UI { ... }
```

The Push annotation accepts two optional parameters: value and transport.The first one, value, configures the *push mode* to use. There are two main options: PushMode.AUTOMATIC and PushMode.MANUAL. AUTOMATIC means all changes to the UI are automatically sent to the client once the UI.access method finishes (technically, once the session lock is released). MANUAL means you have to call UI.push to make the UI changes available in the browser. The second parameter, transport, configures the *transport type* to use. There are three options: Transport.WEBSOCKET (which uses the standard *WebSockets* protocol, a different protocol than HTTP, for all communications between the server and the client), Transport.WEBSOCKET_XHR (which uses WebSockets for server-to-client communication and XHR for client-to-server communication), and Transport.LONG_POLLING (a technique that uses the standard HTTP protocol where the client requests the server for data, the server holds the request until new data is available, and the process is repeated again).

You also have to enable the asynchronous operation mode for the VaadinServlet in order to optimize resources and allow XHR as a fallback mechanism when WebSockets is not available:

```
@WebServlet(value = "/*", asyncSupported = true)
@VaadinServletConfiguration(ui = VaadinUI.class, productionMode = false)
public static class chapter08VaadinServlet extends VaadinServlet {
}
```

Summary

In this chapter, we learned how to render `JasperReports` in Vaadin applications. We used `DynamicJasper`, which allowed us to use the Java Programming Language to design the reports. We also learned how to generate a report in a background thread running on the server and notify the client once the report is ready by using Server Push.

In the next chapter, you will learn about how to handle large volumes of data in UIs by using lazy loading.

9
Lazy Loading

Lazy loading is a technique for lowering memory consumption and, possibly, processing time. This technique delays the loading of data until the moment when it's actually needed in the UI. For example, if you have a `Grid` component with, say 10,000 rows, only a bunch of them are visible at a given time. Loading the full set of 10,000 rows might be a waste of resources. The idea behind lazy loading is the same as the behavior of a lazy person: if you delay doing something until the last moment, you will end up saving time if, for some reason, it turns out that you don't have to do the task anymore. It's the same in a web application. For example, if a user leaves certain views without scrolling through the data, the application won't need to load anything other than a few visible items, saving it from having to load potentially thousands or millions of items from the data source; something that could become a serious problem when many users are on the same view at the same time.

In this chapter, we will discuss how to implement lazy loading with the `Grid` component. However, the same principles apply to any other kind of UI components that show data from large datasets.

This chapter covers the following topics:

- Adding lazy loading capabilities to backend services
- Implementing a `DataProvider` with lambda expressions
- Filtering
- Ordering
- Infinite lazy loading

Technical requirements

You will be required to have Java SE Development Kit and Java EE SDK version 8 or later. You also need Maven version 3 or later. A Java IDE with Maven support, such as IntelliJ IDEA, Eclipse, or NetBeans is recommended. Finally, to use the Git repository of this book, you need to install Git.

The code files of this chapter can be found on GitHub:
`https://github.com/PacktPublishing/Data-centric-Applications-with-Vaadin-8/tree/master/chapter-09`

Check out the following video to see the code in action:
`https://goo.gl/GLTkjq`

The example application

We will develop a simple application to test Vaadin's capability to show hundreds of thousands of rows in a `Grid` component. The users can filter the data in the `Grid` by typing a filter text that the application matches against three of the columns (**Client**, **Phone Number**, and **City**). The users can also change the position of the columns (by dragging them from the header) and order the rows (by clicking on the column headers). The following is a screenshot of the example application:

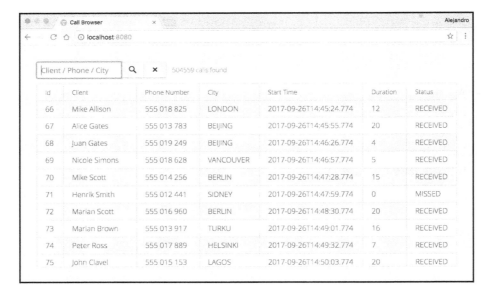

The data model

This chapter uses the same data model used in Chapter 8, *Adding Reporting Capabilities*. The data model is based on a simple SQL table, Call. We'll use JPA to connect to a file-based H2 database. The JPA logic is encapsulated in a CallRepository class. For more details about the data model, please refer to Chapter 8, *Adding Reporting Capabilities*.

 You can find the complete source code of this chapter's example in the Data-centric-Applications-with-Vaadin-8\chapter-09 Maven project of the source code that accompanies this book.

The Vaadin UI

VaadinServlet is configured in the WebConfig class. The UI implementation is realized in the VaadinUI class. For reference, the following is the implementation of the VaadinUI class:

```
@Title("Call Browser")
public class VaadinUI extends UI {

    @Override
    protected void init(VaadinRequest vaadinRequest) {
        VerticalLayout mainLayout = new VerticalLayout();
        mainLayout.addComponentsAndExpand(new CallsBrowser());
        setContent(mainLayout);
    }
}
```

Notice how the UI consists of a VerticalLayout that contains only a CallsBrowser component. We'll start with the following implementation of the CallsBrowser custom component:

```
public class CallsBrowser extends Composite {

    public CallsBrowser() {
        TextField filter = new TextField();
        filter.setPlaceholder("Client / Phone / City");
        filter.focus();

        Button search = new Button(VaadinIcons.SEARCH);
        search.setClickShortcut(ShortcutAction.KeyCode.ENTER);
```

```
        Button clear = new Button(VaadinIcons.CLOSE_SMALL);

        CssLayout filterLayout = new CssLayout(filter, search, clear);
        filterLayout.addStyleName(ValoTheme.LAYOUT_COMPONENT_GROUP);

        Label countLabel = new Label();
        countLabel.addStyleNames(
                ValoTheme.LABEL_LIGHT, ValoTheme.LABEL_SMALL);

        HorizontalLayout headerLayout = new HorizontalLayout(
                filterLayout, countLabel);
        headerLayout.setComponentAlignment(countLabel,
    Alignment.MIDDLE_LEFT);

        Grid<Call> grid = new Grid<>(Call.class);
        grid.setColumns("id", "client", "phoneNumber", "city", "startTime",
                "duration", "status");
        grid.setSizeFull();

        VerticalLayout mainLayout = new VerticalLayout(headerLayout);
        mainLayout.setMargin(false);
        mainLayout.addComponentsAndExpand(grid);
        setCompositionRoot(mainLayout);
    }
}
```

The previous class can be used as a starting point if you want to implement the concepts of this chapter yourself. At this point, the UI doesn't show any data in the Grid and it has no behavior.

Preparing the backend for lazy loading

Lazy loading (and filtering) capabilities should be delegated to the backend as much as possible. Although the Grid class itself is able to cache some of the data and send it to the client only when needed, it cannot prevent you from querying the whole database, for example. In order to support lazy loading, backend services should provide the means to lazily load the data.

Typically, the UI gets the data from a service or repository class. Let's see an example of how a repository class can provide methods with lazy loading capabilities. The CallRepository class could define a findAll method that queries a *slice* of the rows in the Call table, as follows:

```
public class CallRepository {

    public static List<Call> findAll(int offset, int limit) {
        ...
    }

    public static int count() {
        ...
    }
}
```

In the previous code, limit is used to *limit* the number of rows (actually, instances of User) that should be returned. When using SQL, this can be used as the LIMIT clause in a SQL query. offset is used to *skip* a number of rows, which is equivalent to the starting row number. For example, if the SQL table has 100 rows, and we use offset=10 and limit=5, the method should return only the rows 10 to 15. If we use offset=98 and limit=5, the method should return rows 98 to 100 (there are not enough rows left after 98 to complete a set of five rows).

For reference, here's what a JPA implementation of these methods could look like:

```
public class CallRepository {
    ...

    public static List<Call> find(int offset, int limit) {
        return JPAService.runInTransaction(em -> {
            Query query = em.createQuery("select c from Call c");
            query.setFirstResult(offset);
            query.setMaxResults(limit);

            List<Call> resultList = query.getResultList();
            return resultList;
        });
    }

    public static int count() {
        return JPAService.runInTransaction(em -> {
            Query query = em.createQuery("select count(c.id) from Call c");

            Long count = (Long) query.getSingleResult();
            return count.intValue();
```

```
            });
        }
    }
```

Notice how we included a `count` method in the previous snippet of code. This is required in some situations, such as when using lazy loading with the `Grid` component.

Lazy loading with the Grid component

A `Grid` component can take advantage of the `offset` and `limit` parameters described in the previous section by using the `setDataProvider` method, as follows:

```
grid.setDataProvider(
    (sortOrders, offset, limit) ->
            CallRepository.findAll(offset, limit).stream(),
    () -> CallRepository.count()
);
```

The previous code defines two lambda expressions:

- `(sortOrders, offset, limit) -> service.find(...)`: This lambda expression should return all the items used in *slice* defined by the `offset` and `limit` parameters (we will see how to use the `sortOrders` parameters later)
- `() -> service.count()`: This lambda expression should return the total count of items available with no *slices*

The `setDataProvider` method we used in the previous example receives an instance of `FetchItemsCallback`, a functional interface that defines a method to fetch the items (or rows):

```
@FunctionalInterface
public interface FetchItemsCallback<T> extends Serializable {

    public Stream<T> fetchItems(
            List<QuerySortOrder> sortOrder, int offset, int limit);
}
```

You can also use another version of the `setDataProvider` method that accepts an instance of `DataProvider`. There's a static helper method in the `DataProvider` interface that allows you to implement it from lambda expressions similar to the ones we used before:

```
DataProvider<Call, Void> dataProvider = DataProvider.fromCallbacks(
        query -> CallRepository.find(
```

```
                        query.getOffset(),
                        query.getLimit()).stream(),
                query -> CallRepository.count()
);

grid.setDataProvider(dataProvider);
```

The difference with the previous version is that we get the offset and limit values from a Query instance, so we need to use the corresponding getters.

Adding filters

Filtering should be done with the help of backend services as well. We can implement this in the same way as we did in Chapter 7, *Implementing CRUD User Interfaces*. First, the backend service method should accept the filter input. In the example application, the filter value is a String, but in other situations, you may need a custom object containing all the values that can be used for filtering. Here is the new find method, which accepts a filter String:

```
public static List<Call> find(int offset, int limit, String filter,
        Map<String, Boolean> sort) {
    return JPAService.runInTransaction(em -> {
        Query query = em.createQuery("select c from Call c where
lower(c.client) like :filter or c.phoneNumber like :filter or lower(c.city)
like :filter");
        query.setParameter("filter",
                "%" + filter.trim().toLowerCase() + "%");
        query.setFirstResult(offset);
        query.setMaxResults(limit);

        List<Call> resultList = query.getResultList();
        return resultList;
    });
}
```

Notice how we make the filter case-insensitive by using the lower JPQL function and converting the filter value to lowercase using the toLowerCase method. We are also using the % operator to allow matches in the middle of the values in the database. We have to do something similar with the count method:

```
public static int count(String filter) {
    return JPAService.runInTransaction(em -> {
        Query query = em.createQuery("select count(c.id) from Call c where
lower(c.client) like :filter or c.phoneNumber like :filter or lower(c.city)
```

```
like :filter");
        query.setParameter("filter", "%" + filter.trim().toLowerCase() +
"%");

        Long count = (Long) query.getSingleResult();
        return count.intValue();
    });
}
```

On the UI side of the implementation, we need to send the filter value to the service method. This value comes from the `filter` text field:

```
DataProvider<Call, Void> dataProvider =
DataProvider.fromFilteringCallbacks(
        query -> CallRepository.find(query.getOffset(), query.getLimit(),
            filter.getValue()).stream(),
        query -> CallRepository.count(filter.getValue())
);
```

We also need to refresh the `DataProvider` when the **Search** button is clicked. This can be done using a `ClickListener` and the `refreshAll` method of the `DataProvider` interface:

```
search.addClickListener(e -> dataProvider.refreshAll());
```

Something similar can be done for the `clear` button, which removes the filter introduced by the user:

```
clear.addClickListener(e -> {
    filter.clear();
    dataProvider.refreshAll();
});
```

When the `refreshAll` method is invoked, the lambda expressions we previously defined are called again and the new data is fetched from the service class.

It's generally a good idea to add database indexes to the columns the application uses to filter data. In the example application, we allow filtering on the `client`, `phoneNumber`, and `city` columns. You can let JPA create these indexes by using the `@Index` annotation, as follows:

```
@Entity
@Table(indexes = {
        @Index(name = "client_index", columnList = "client"),
        @Index(name = "phoneNumber_index", columnList = "phoneNumber"),
        @Index(name = "city_index", columnList = "city")
```

```
})
@Data
public class Call {
    ...
}
```

By default, the example application generates around 500,000 rows in the `Call` table. Unfortunately, the `Grid` class cannot handle this amount of rows. See the following issues on GitHub for more information about these limitations: `https://github.com/vaadin/framework/issues/6290`, and `https://github.com/vaadin/framework/issues/9751`. One way to overcome these issues is by making the filter show results in the `Grid` only when the number of rows the query returns is less than an established threshold.

Ordering rows in Grid components

As you can guess, ordering (or sorting) is another task that should be delegated to the backend services when possible. Moreover, it is most likely required when you are implementing pagination (that is, lazy loading using `limit` and `offset` parameters) in the backend service as well.

The service method should include a parameter that specifies how to perform the ordering. The `Grid` component allows users to click on the column headers to activate ordering by that column. These columns that need ordering are passed to the `DataProvider` in a `Query` object. You can get these by calling the `Query.getSortOrders()` method, which returns a `List` of `QuerySortOrder` objects. You could pass this `List` to the service method, but it's always a good idea to avoid coupling the backend services with frontend technologies. `QuerySortOrder` is a class included in Vaadin Framework, so you would need to include Vaadin dependencies in your backend services if they are deployed in a separate artifact, for example. To avoid this coupling, we can implement a utility method that converts between `QuerySortOrder` objects to framework-independent objects. In the backend services, we can use a `Map<String, Boolean>`, where the key is a `String` containing the name of the property, and the value is a `Boolean` that tells the method whether to order in an ascending mode or not.

Preparing the backend services

Let's start, then, by adding a parameter for the ordering configuration to the `find` method of the `CallRepository` in the example application:

```
public static List<Call> find(int offset, int limit,
        String filter, Map<String, Boolean> order) {
    return JPAService.runInTransaction(em -> {
        String jpql = "select c from Call c where lower(c.client) like
:filter or c.phoneNumber like :filter or lower(c.city) like :filter" +
buildOrderByClause(sort);
        Query query = em.createQuery(jpql);
        query.setParameter("filter", "%" + filter.trim().toLowerCase() +
"%");

        query.setFirstResult(offset);
        query.setMaxResults(limit);

        List<Call> resultList = query.getResultList();
        return resultList;
    });
}
```

The `order` parameter contains the name of the properties we need to sort by. We need to convert this `Map` to an `order by` clause (in a `String` form) in JPQL. This is done in the `buildOrderByClause` method:

```
private static String buildOrderByClause(Map<String, Boolean> order) {
    StringBuilder orderBy = new StringBuilder();
    order.forEach((property, isAscending) -> orderBy.append(property +
(isAscending ? "" : " desc") + ","));

    if (orderBy.length() > 0) {
        orderBy.delete(orderBy.length() - 1, orderBy.length());
        return " order by " + orderBy.toString();
    } else {
        return "";
    }
}
```

If the user clicks the **Client** header in the `Grid`, the `buildOrderByClause` method will return the following string:

```
" order by client"
```

This string would be concatenated to the end of the JPQL query, which in turn would be executed in the `find` method.

The `Grid` component also supports ordering by multiple columns. To add a column to the order configuration, users have to press and hold the *Shift* key down while clicking the column header. For example, if the user clicks the **Client** header and presses and holds the *Shift* key down while clicking the **City** header, the `buildOrderByClause` method would return the following string:

```
" order by client,city"
```

Enabling ordering in the UI

As we have previously discussed, the `DataProvider` interface uses an object of type `List<QuerySortOrder>` to provide the ordering configuration. However, the backend service requires an object of type `Map<String, Boolean>`. We have to implement a helper method that translates between these two types. We can add this method to a separate `DataUtils` class and implement it as follows:

```
public class DataUtils {

    public static <T, F> Map<String, Boolean> getOrderMap(
            Query<T, F> query) {
        Map<String, Boolean> map = new LinkedHashMap<>();

        for (QuerySortOrder order : query.getSortOrders()) {
            String property = order.getSorted();
            boolean isAscending = SortDirection.ASCENDING.equals(
                    order.getDirection());
            map.put(property, isAscending);
        }

        return map;
    }
}
```

The `getOrderMap` method iterates over the `QuerySortOrder` objects returned by the `query.getSortOrders()` method and maps them to entries in a map of type `Map<String, Boolean>`. Notice how we used the `LinkedHasMap` type. This allows us to keep the entries in the map in the same order in which they come from the `List` provided by the `query` object, something we need if we want to support multiple-column ordering in the `Grid` (the `order by` clause should reflect the sequence used when the user clicked the headers in the browser).

We can use this utility method in the `DataProvider`, as follows:

```
DataProvider<Call, Void> dataProvider =
DataProvider.fromFilteringCallbacks(
        query -> CallRepository.find(query.getOffset(), query.getLimit(),
    filter.getValue(), DataUtils.getOrderMap(query)).stream(),
        query -> {
            int count = CallRepository.count(filter.getValue());
            countLabel.setValue(count + " calls found");
            return count;
        }
);
```

The final result is illustrated in the following screenshot:

To complete this chapter's example, we can enable column reordering (the users can drag the columns in the browser to reposition them) as follows:

```
grid.setColumnReorderingAllowed(true);
```

UX and large datasets

To close this chapter, let me share some thoughts about the convenience (or inconvenience) of having a `Grid` with 10,000 (or more) rows in it.

Lazy loading Grid versus direct search

In the screen I'm using to develop the examples of this chapter, I can see around 15 rows at a time in a `Grid` component. If I want to see the row 5,390, for example, I have to scroll down and try to find the rows around 5,390. That takes me 1 or 2 seconds if I'm lucky. After this, I have to do some fine-tuned scrolling to get to the exact row. Something that can take 1 or 2 seconds again. This scrolling-through to search data is possible with this example application because the demo data is generated with consecutive numbers for the values in the fields. There are no missing numbers. In other situations, this might not be possible at all. Even in the cases where this is possible, scrolling through thousands of rows is not a good user experience.

Filters aim to help; clicking on a `TextField` and typing 5,390 is faster than scrolling through the data. However, if the user is supposed to type 5,390, we could argue that rendering thousands of rows is not even required. The whole UI could potentially be redesigned to better fit the use case. When you encounter this kind of `Grid` with thousands of rows in it, put yourself in others' shoes; in the users' shoes. Consider wizard-like interfaces, infinite lazy loading on scroll (like Facebook or Twitter), or any other event, and splitting the view into several views, each one for a more specific use case.

Infinite lazy loading

Even though we have explained lazy loading by using the `Grid` component, we can use the same backend service method to implement custom UI components that support lazy loading. For example, you can use a `VerticalLayout` to add sets of, say, 10 components any time the user clicks a *load more* button at the bottom of the layout. In this case, you would need to keep track of the current offset and keep incrementing it until the service method returns less than 10 items.

The following is a simple UI component that shows how to implement this type of infinite lazy loading:

```
public class LazyLoadingVerticalLayout extends Composite {

    private CssLayout content = new CssLayout();
    private Button button = new Button("Load more...");

    private int offset;
    private int pageSize;

    public LazyLoadingVerticalLayout(int pageSize) {
        this.pageSize = pageSize;

        button.setStyleName(ValoTheme.BUTTON_BORDERLESS_COLORED);

        VerticalLayout mainLayout = new VerticalLayout(content, button);
        setCompositionRoot(mainLayout);

        button.addClickListener(e -> loadMore());
        loadMore();
    }

    public void loadMore() {
        List<Call> calls = CallRepository.find(
                offset, pageSize, "", new HashMap<>());

        if (calls.size() < pageSize) {
            button.setVisible(false);
        }

        calls.stream()
                .map(call -> new Label(call.toString()))
                .forEach(content::addComponent);

        offset += pageSize;
    }
}
```

Notice how the loadMore method keeps adding components to the content layout until there are no more results to add, at which point the **Load more...** button is hidden from the UI.

The following screenshot shows this component in action:

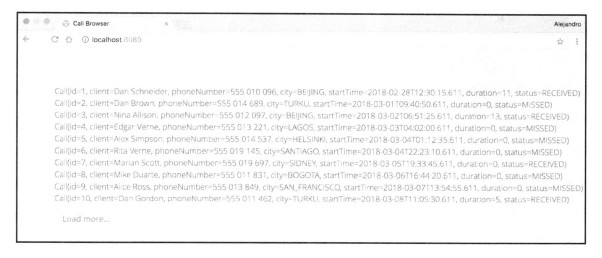

Summary

In this chapter, we learned how to implement lazy loading by enhancing the backend service methods to support it. We learned how to use a lazy-loaded `Grid` component with filtering and ordering capabilities. We implemented a `DataProvider` by providing two lambda expressions: one for getting slices of data and one for counting the total number of items. We also discussed UX aspects to take into consideration when dealing with large datasets and learned how to implement infinite lazy loading as an alternative to having a `Grid` with thousands of rows.

This chapter closes the journey through many interesting topics related to modularization, API design, UI design, and data management in applications developed with Vaadin. There is much more to this subjects that we cannot cover in this book. Hopefully, this book inspired you to find good solutions to some of the challenges you may encounter when developing data-centric web applications with Vaadin. Happy coding!

Other Books You May Enjoy

If you enjoyed this book, you may be interested in these other books by Packt:

Building Web Apps with Spring 5 and Angular
Ajitesh Shukla

ISBN: 978-1-78728-466-1

- Set up development environment for Spring Web App and Angular app
- Process web request and response and build REST API endpoints
- Create data access components using Spring Web MVC framework and Hibernate
- Use Junit 5 to test your application
- Learn the fundamental concepts around building Angular
- Configure and use Routes and Components
- Protect Angular app content from common web vulnerabilities and attacks
- Integrate Angular apps with Spring Boot Web API endpoints
- Deploy the web application based on CI and CD using Jenkins and Docker containers

Full Stack Development with JHipster
Deepu K Sasidharan, Sendil Kumar N

ISBN:978-1-78847-631-7

- Build business logic by creating and developing entity models us the JHipster Domain Language
- Customize web applications with Angular, Bootstrap and Spring
- Tests and Continuous Integration with Jenkins
- Utilize the JHipster microservice stack, which includes Netflix Eureka, Spring Cloud config, HashiCorp Consul, and so on
- Understand advanced microservice concepts such as API rout, load balancing, rate limit, circuit break, centralized configuration server, JWT authentication, and more
- Run microservices locally using Docker and Kubernetes (in production)

Leave a review - let other readers know what you think

Please share your thoughts on this book with others by leaving a review on the site that you bought it from. If you purchased the book from Amazon, please leave us an honest review on this book's Amazon page. This is vital so that other potential readers can see and use your unbiased opinion to make purchasing decisions, we can understand what our customers think about our products, and our authors can see your feedback on the title that they have worked with Packt to create. It will only take a few minutes of your time, but is valuable to other potential customers, our authors, and Packt. Thank you!

Index

W